CHER HAMPTON

Codependency Recovery Workbook

9 Steps to Overcome Fear of Abandonment, Stop Pleasing People & Develop Healthy Relationships

Copyright © 2023 by Cher Hampton

All rights reserved. No part of this publication may be reproduced, stored or transmitted in any form or by any means, electronic, mechanical, photocopying, recording, scanning, or otherwise without written permission from the publisher. It is illegal to copy this book, post it to a website, or distribute it by any other means without permission.

Under no circumstances will any blame or legal responsibility be held against the publisher, or author, for any damages, reparation, or monetary loss due to the information contained within this book, either directly or indirectly.

Disclaimer Notice:

Please note the information contained within this document is for educational and entertainment purposes only. All effort has been executed to present accurate, up to date, reliable, complete information. No warranties of any kind are declared or implied. Readers acknowledge that the author is not engaged in the rendering of legal, financial, medical or professional advice. The content within this book has been derived from various sources. Please consult a licensed professional before attempting any techniques outlined in this book.

By reading this document, the reader agrees that under no circumstances is the author responsible for any losses, direct or indirect, that are incurred as a result of the use of the information contained within this document, including, but not limited to, errors, omissions, or inaccuracies.

First edition

This book was professionally typeset on Reedsy. Find out more at reedsy.com

Contents

BONUS: Your Free Gifts	vi
Introduction	ix
How to Use This Book	x
1 Define Codependency	1
What Is Codependency?	1
The Stages of Codependent Relationships	6
Four Stages of Codependency Recovery	9
Exercise: Are You a Giver?	12
2 Understand the Risk Factors	14
What Causes Codependency?	14
Trauma and Codependency	15
Mental Illness and Codependency	19
Attachment and Codependency	21
Dysfunctional Families and Codependency	27
3 Recognize How Codependency Looks In Different Relationships	36
Recognizing Codependency in Different Relationships	36
Codependency in Romantic Relationships	38
Codependency in Parent-Child Relationships	42
Codependency in Friendships	46
Codependency in Work Relationships	50
Exercises to Become a Better Version of You	54
4 End the Terror of Obsessive Thinking	73
What Does Obsession Have to Do With Codependency?	73
Obsessive Love Disorder	78

	Confronting Obsessive Thinking With the Four Stages of Codependency Recovery	82
5	Put Yourself First and Set Boundaries	90
	Early Childhood and Boundaries	90
	The Need to Address Boundary Violations	92
	Examples of Boundary Violations and How to Repair Them	94
	Why You Should Put Yourself First	100
	Exercise: Self-Care Checklist	103
6	Learn the Art of Assertive Communication	106
	What It Means to Be a People-Pleaser	106
	How Codependency Affects Communication	108
	Strategies to Communicate Assertively	111
7	Improve Your Relationship With Fear	116
	Is Fear the Real Enemy?	116
	Healing From Codependency Fears	118
	Conquering the Fear of Rejection	119
	Overcome Your Limiting Beliefs	121
	The Power in Accepting Your Fears	126
	Exercise: Processing Fears With Inner Child Work	127
8	Decide to Stay or Leave	132
	Can Codependent Relationships Work?	132
	Five-Step Plan to Leave a Codependent Relationship	137
	Managing Post-Breakup Grief	140
9	Celebrate This New Chapter	144
	What Are You Looking Forward To?	144
	Nurture Your Close Relationships	148
	How to Manage the First Healthy Romantic Relationship	150
	Rewrite Your Life Story	153
	Strengthen Your Relationship With the Divine	156
Conclusion		161

BONUS: Your Free Gifts	164
Thank You	167
References	169

BONUS: Your Free Gifts

I'm only offering this bonus for FREE to my readers. This is a way of saying thanks for your purchase. In this gift, you will find a self-development course to give your inner journey a head start.

The Personality Development Wisdom Course

Master the Art of Becoming the Best Version of Yourself for **Ultimate Succes and Growth!**

Inside this course, you will find:

1. Personality Development - An Overview
2. How to Transform Yourself into a Better Version
3. How To Improve Your Body Language
4. How to Boost Up Your Self-Confidence, Self-Esteem, and Motivation
5. Best Tips to Overcome Procrastination
6. The Power of Positive Thinking
7. How to Improve Your Workplace Wellness
8. How to Enhance Your Softskill
9. Learn and Practice the Art of Work-Life Balance
10. How to Deal With Failures
11. How to Manage and Overcome Your Fears
12. Best Ways to Deal With Difficult People
13. Stress and Energy Management
14. How to Have a Productive Day
15. Bonus 1 - Cheat Sheet
16. Bonus 2 - Mind Map
17. Bonus 3 - Top Resource Report
18. Bonus 4 - 10 Extra Articles

To receive this extra **bonus,** go to: https://booksforbetterlife.com/codependency-recovery-workbook

Or scan the QR code:

Introduction

"Many of us live in denial of who we truly are because we fear losing someone or something—and there are times that if we don't rock the boat, too often the one we lose is ourselves."

— DENNIS MERRITT JONES

Codependency is commonly seen as one of the harmful behaviors that threaten healthy relationships and creates a dysfunctional dynamic. In codependent relationships, the couple, parent-child, or best friends take on two different roles: the sacrificial giver and the unapologetic taker.

The sacrificial giver downplays their needs at the expense of responding to the needs of the other. Due to a number of factors, such as their early childhood attachments, or preconceived ideas about love, they derive a sense of self-worth from proving themselves to others.

The unapologetic taker tends to also struggle with issues of self-worth, and relies significantly on the support, affection, and responsiveness of the other person to have a stable sense of self. The only difference is that instead of giving endless amounts of reassurance, they take as much as they can get.

Codependency isn't a new term, and many of us are aware of the damage of losing ourselves in service to others. However, as common as this relationship dynamic is, we often find it difficult to recognize the signs of codependent relationships, or realize what we can do to break the cycle.

Take my life, for example. Growing up, I thought that the codependent relationship with my mother was normal. From as early as I can remember, my mother suffered from bipolar disorder and would often require more caretaking, as opposed to providing nurturing and support. But this didn't seem out of the ordinary. After all, wasn't it every child's responsibility to take care of their parents?

It was only when I reached a state of burnout and suffered from depression in my teen years that I realized how unhealthy our mother-daughter relationship dynamic had been. The constant giving that felt like love was actually a sign of a lack of boundaries and deep-rooted insecurities. But since healthy displays of affection and nurturing were not modeled in front of me as a child, it wasn't an easy process confronting our dysfunctional relationship—and the codependent personality I had developed.

How to Use This Book

As a psychologist today, I see many clients who desire to learn how to break cycles of codependency. Fortunately for them, they have already recognized the dysfunctional pattern in their relationships, but they still lack the proper psychological tools to build a solid sense of self, separate their needs from others' needs, and strive for independence rather than codependence.

As part of their therapeutic intervention, I take them through the codependency recovery plan, which consists of nine steps to gradually heal from this relationship dynamic and prioritize their well-being. The nine steps include:

- Chapter 1: Define Codependency
- Chapter 2: Understand the Risk Factors
- Chapter 3: Recognize How Codependency Looks in Different Relationships
- Chapter 4: End the Terror of Obsessive Thinking
- Chapter 5: Put Yourself First and Set Boundaries
- Chapter 6: Learn the Art of Assertive Communication
- Chapter 7: Improve Your Relationship With Fear
- Chapter 8: Decide to Stay or Leave
- Chapter 9: Celebrate This New Chapter

The purpose of this book is to teach the above steps from my own experiences with codependency, and what I have learned over the years as a trained psychologist. By the end of the book, you will be able to explain what codependency is, how the dynamic is formed, and implement various strategies to break free from the cycle and prioritize self-growth and mutually supportive relationships.

The key to fulfilling relationships, as I have learned, is to cultivate psychological safety and create a space where both parties feel comfortable to show up as they are. Unconditional acceptance of the other is the secret ingredient that keeps two imperfect people connected and thriving within their relationships. Get ready to learn what it means to feel psychologically safe in your relationships and be empowered to express who you are, openly and freely!

1

Define Codependency

"Once they have been affected—once "it" sets in—codependency takes on a life of its own. It is similar to catching pneumonia or picking up a destructive habit. Once you've got it, you've got it."

— MELODY BEATTIE

What Is Codependency?

Historically, the term *codependency* was used to describe the relationship dynamic between substance abusers and members of their family. Codependent behaviors were synonymous with supportive behaviors, even though they were simply an act of enabling the behaviors of the addict.

There is nothing "supportive" about codependent relationships. At the core, you have two individuals who do not have a stable sense of self, and as a result, they rely significantly on each other to fulfill their physical, mental, and emotional needs.

Codependent relationships tend to be intimate and long-lasting, like any other healthy relationship. However, due to both individuals defining themselves based on their relationship, the attachment formed is not liberating, nor does it support trust, individuality, or accountability.

The pair will do whatever it takes to stay together, even if it means overlooking boundaries, forgetting about their individual interests and needs, and turning a blind eye to dysfunctional behaviors.

This leads to the next point. To sustain a codependent relationship, both parties need to play a different role. One person becomes the giver and the other the taker. How the roles are chosen depends on a number of factors, such as the personality of each person, how each defines love and attachment, as well as what each person's core needs are.

The giver, for example, is typically an empathetic person, who defines love by the measure of caretaking they can offer another person. They may also believe that they are responsible for "fixing" others or making them happy. The giver feels anxious when their loved one is upset or distant, and may blame themselves for their loved one's bad moods or unloving behaviors. Deep down, the giver fears being abandoned, and they will do whatever it takes to protect the relationship.

On the other hand, the taker is typically an insecure person, who defines love by the measure of validation they can receive from another person. They may display a sense of entitlement in relationships, believing that they deserve to be loved, protected, and nurtured. It is common to find that takers suffer from some sort of mental health condition, whether it be a form of addiction, mood disorder, or personality disorder.

Due to their condition, they lack the awareness required to recognize the excessive giving and self-sacrificing behaviors of the giver, or the desire to set healthy limits and practice reciprocity.

It is important to mention that codependent relationships begin with good intentions. Both the giver and taker are attracted to each other because of how each person is able to respond to the other's core needs. The giver fears being alone and, therefore, needs the presence of the taker to feel secure. The taker fears being unlovable and, therefore, needs ample amounts of validation from the giver to feel secure.

What makes codependent relationships unhealthy is the level of denial that both parties will go to in order to keep the relationship together. This tends to open the relationship up to all sorts of dysfunctional behaviors and abuse, which can lead to anxiety, low self-esteem, depression, and a sense of helplessness.

What Codependency Is and Isn't

Codependency is often misunderstood as relying on your loved one to respond to your needs. The truth is there is nothing wrong with having needs, communicating them, and taking turns to respond to each other's needs.

What makes a relationship healthy is the level of emotional interdependence that exists between a couple, parent and child, or best friends. Emotional interdependence is a term used to describe the capacity of both individuals to empathize and emotionally lean on one another. It is normal and healthy, for example, to need quality time, words of affirmation, acts of service, physical touch, and gift giving from your loved one, and for them to expect those same needs to be met.

Individuals in codependent relationships don't show a lot of emotional interdependence. The relationship is normally skewed toward prioritizing the needs of one person—the taker—causing inequality and dependency. Furthermore, the giver tends to regard their needs as being less important and urgent than the needs of the other person.

Unlike healthy relationships where both individuals find value in the union, codependent relationships are often kept going by the giver. The giver invests so much time and energy in maintaining the relationship, to the detriment of their health, career, and social relationships.

For example, the giver is less likely to have hobbies, a strong support network, or personal goals outside the relationship, whereas the taker may enjoy a full and enriching life outside the relationship.

Below are a few more patterns that the giver may display in a codependent relationship:

- **Being in denial of the state of their relationship.** The giver may struggle to recognize or accept what they are feeling. Even when they can sense that the relationship dynamic is unhealthy, they might distort reality, like believing it is selfish to not respond to every need of the taker.
- **Having a low self-esteem.** The giver has a deep fear of standing on their own. This fear makes it hard for them to make decisions, express their thoughts and feelings, or ask for what they need. Moreover, they may have a low sense of self-worth, and doubt that anybody may find them worthy of receiving love.
- **Compromising on their needs to a fault.** There are limits to how much you can give in any healthy relationships. In most cases, the limits are determined by your own physical and emotional

boundaries. Since the giver doesn't have firm boundaries, they tend to compromise their values and engage in people-pleasing behaviors to avoid rejection or the taker's aggression.

- **Display controlling behaviors.** The giver derives a sense of satisfaction from taking care of others. However, if they are not careful, it could lead to controlling behaviors, like insisting on others taking their help, trying to persuade others to accept their ideas, using sex to gain acceptance, or finding other covert ways to influence others.
- **Avoiding behaviors that might bring shame or rejection from others.** Due to the deep-rooted fear of rejection, the giver may avoid actions that could open them up to being ridiculed, shamed, or judged by others. For instance, they might avoid emotional intimacy in relationships, or attempt to hide their emotions altogether because emotions are perceived as a sign of weakness.
- **Struggling to enforce healthy boundaries.** Both the giver and taker may struggle to recognize, respect, and enforce boundaries in their relationships. From the giver's perspective, they may not insist on boundaries out of fear of backlash from the other person. They may have a hard time asserting themselves and calling out bad behavior when it happens.
- **Insisting on taking care of others.** It is normal to have the desire to take care of loved ones, but not to the extent of worrying about them, or obsessing about how they choose to live their lives. In some cases, the giver is groomed into the role of caretaker as a child by their parents. For example, affection may be withheld whenever the child doesn't respond to their parent's needs. They may grow up believing that something bad will happen if they don't devote themselves to taking care of loved ones
- **Struggling to communicate openly.** Codependent relationships

naturally breed a lack, or poor communication. From the giver's perspective, they may fear expressing their needs, and end up using passive ways of communicating with others. Even when they are frustrated, the giver would much rather internalize their anger, and blame themselves, rather than confronting the issue at hand.

The Stages of Codependent Relationships

Codependency doesn't form overnight in a relationship. It often unfolds in a number of stages, which could take years to fully develop. There are generally three stages of codependency: the early stage, middle stage, and late stage. When the patterns of codependent behavior are not addressed, the dynamic of the relationship becomes progressively worse. Understanding each stage of codependency can help you identify some of your codependent traits and just how enmeshed you are in your relationship.

Below is a breakdown of the three stages of codependency:

The Early Stage

The first stage is very difficult to identify because it looks like any other loving relationship. Both parties display a lot of affection toward each other, and are able and willing to respond to each other's needs. The subtle difference between the parties is in how they define the relationship, and how they view each other.

The giver, for example, will likely fantasize about the taker. If they are in a romantic relationship, the giver will believe that they have found their soulmate, whereas if it is a parent-child relationship, the giver (could be the child or parent) will have an immense amount of admiration for the other person.

The taker may care about the giver too; however, they are more likely to have a balanced view about the relationship and the other person. They are aware of the giver's pleasant and unpleasant traits, and will therefore see them realistically.

Naturally, both parties in the codependent relationship will start to spend less time with their friends or family, or lose interest in many of their hobbies. The difference between the giver and the taker, though, is that after some time, the taker will regain a sense of individuality and reconnect with their friends or family. The giver, on the other hand, will not.

The Middle Stage

By nature, healthy relationships are built on reciprocity. What this means is that both partners take turns giving and taking. It isn't necessarily a titt-for-tatt scenario, but more so the awareness of how much each person contributes to the well-being of the other.

Codependent relationships do not have a strong foundation of reciprocity. This becomes more noticeable during the middle stage. The major factor to look out for here is the amount of time and effort both parties invest in the relationship.

It is common to find the giver making more compromises for their needs and lifestyle than the taker. They may not always enjoy being the one who is always bending their boundaries; however, it is seen as a small price to pay for maintaining the relationship.

The taker, who may be self-absorbed or oblivious to the needs of their loved one, may start to request certain treatment or norms in the relationship. They may not always stop to empathize with the giver and recognize just how much they are already investing into the relationship. Expecting unconditional love, nurturing, and cooperation becomes an unrealistic expectation for the taker.

To maintain the status quo of their relationship, the taker may develop unpleasant behaviors, like constantly nagging or guilt-tripping their loved one, in order to have their needs met. In extreme cases, some takers may even go as far as using manipulation tactics to keep their loved one constantly focused on their well-being.

Not all people in codependent relationships are ignorant of the power imbalance and lack of reciprocity. For instance, the giver may notice that their needs always take the back seat, but how they respond isn't the same as someone in a healthy relationship. Instead of sitting down with the other person, sharing their concerns, and setting boundaries, they might fight back with passive-aggressive tactics, like giving the silent treatment or performing subtle acts of sabotage.

When questioned by outsiders about the state of their relationship, they might lie to protect the taker from any backlash. Alternatively, they may withdraw from friends and family or find mind-numbing distractions or obsessions to avoid doing something about their unhealthy relationship dynamic.

The Late Stage

When codependency issues are left unaddressed, they may start to affect the giver's physical and mental well-being. Some of the mental health conditions related to codependency include anxiety, depression, and bipolar disorder. On a physical level, givers can also suffer with a host of issues like chronic migraines, loss of appetite, gut problems, insomnia, and eating disorders.

It may come as a surprise to learn that the taker's health suffers too—but not in the way you might expect. Due to the power imbalance in the relationship that favors the taker, they might develop a sense of superiority, entitlement, and hostility when they are being challenged. These are typical characteristics of narcissistic personality disorder, but may also make them vulnerable to other personality disorders.

Four Stages of Codependency Recovery

To avoid reaching the late stage of codependency, it is important to develop a strong sense of self. Throughout this book, you will learn how to do this by learning useful techniques and practicing various exercises.

Whether you are in the early, middle, or late stages of a codependent relationship, please be encouraged that you can retrain your mind on how to relate to others. The secret to this is undertaking the four stages of codependency recovery.

On the following pages is a look at what you can expect at each stage.

Stage 1: Abstinence

You can think of codependency as being similar to an addiction, except the "substance" you are addicted to is another human being. Therefore, the first step in recovery is spending some time away from the other person and refocusing your attention on your personal growth.

If spending some time away is not possible due to family commitments or financial obligations, you can practice detaching from the other person, which might include letting go of the need to control them and feeling personally responsible for their well-being.

The goal of abstinence is to create enough separation between you and the other person, so that you can discover your own beliefs, needs, and feelings. This process isn't easy, regardless of how long you have been with the other codependent person.

In some cases, it may even feel dangerous if the relationship has become abusive. Speaking to people who have recovered from their codependency issues may give you the courage it takes to initiate the separation and focus on yourself.

Stage 2: Awareness

The second step is to reflect on the nature of your relationship. Being separated from the other person will give you enough space to reflect on behaviors you may have never questioned before, like how they insist on having their needs met, but don't respond positively when you make requests.

Be on the lookout for denial or blaming the other person for the state of the relationship. Remember, it takes two to tango. As a giver, there was something that attracted you to the taker, as well as something in them that was attracted to you. The awareness stage is about identifying those internal wounds and beliefs that caused the codependent dynamic in the first place.

Stage 3: Acceptance

At the heart of codependency recovery is acceptance. This could be the acceptance of reality as it is, and the fullness of who you are. For example, one of your personality traits as a giver is being a people-pleaser. This might not be a trait that you have accepted about yourself. The lack of acceptance means that you cannot fully comprehend what being a people-pleaser means or looks like for you, and as a result, you are unable to address people-pleasing behaviors.

Acceptance also involves learning to be enough for yourself. This isn't an easy milestone to reach, since being in a codependent relationship taught you to define who you are based on what others think about you. It will take time to be comfortable being disliked by other people, who may not approve of your opinions, how you live, or the boundaries you create.

Stage 4: Action

The final step is to take action. It isn't enough to gain so much insight about your previous relationships and areas of self-improvement, without putting what you have learned to practice. The three B's—beliefs, behaviors, and boundaries—will be the test to see how much you have understood about yourself.

Taking action will encourage you to step outside your comfort zone, like exploring new types of self-care, getting to know different types of people, or finally living the lifestyle you have always dreamt of. These new experiences will help you get to know yourself better, and positively affect your self-esteem.

Closer to the end of the book, we will take another look at the four stages of codependency recovery, and focus on how you can practice them to manage obsessive tendencies.

Exercise: Are You a Giver?

Even though you have shown interest in the topic of codependency, you may still be wondering whether this relationship dynamic fits your experience. To gain more understanding about the symptoms of a giver, complete the short codependency quiz below.

Read the questions and put a tick inside the columns "Yes" or "No." Please note that the questions refer to a "partner," however, they apply to other types of close relationships too (i.e. friends, parent-child, siblings, etc.).

DEFINE CODEPENDENCY

Questions	Yes	No
Have you ever skipped work to spend time with, or attend to, a false emergency of your partner?		
Has being in the relationship caused you to withdraw from friends and family?		
Have you ever lied to avoid your partner's negative reaction?		
Have you ever manipulated people to do what you want?		
Has being in the relationship caused you to lose sight of your interests and goals?		
After resolving an argument with your partner, do you try to get even?		
Has the thought of leaving the relationship crossed your mind?		
Do you turn a blind eye to your partner's bad habits, addictions, or obsessions?		
Have you ever borrowed your partner's money to get them out of a situation they could have prevented?		
Are you secretly harboring resentment for your partner?		
Has your relationship contributed to the decline of your physical and mental well-being?		
Have you ever felt unlovable?		
Do you often extend yourself to respond to other people's needs, but don't get the same support in return?		
Do you believe that your partner cannot survive without you?		
Would you rather deny your own needs to make others feel comfortable?		
Do you suppress strong emotions because you are afraid of receiving backlash?		

If you have answered "yes" to five or more of these questions, you may display symptoms of codependency in your relationship.

2

Understand the Risk Factors

"Codependency doesn't acknowledge that we actually feel what others are experiencing and want it to stop because it hurts us too."

— JENNIFER ELIZABETH MOORE

What Causes Codependency?

Life is full of ups and downs. If we all took a moment to think about our pasts long enough, we could write down a list of positive and negative events that we have witnessed or been a part of.

But not everybody responds to life's challenges the same way. Perhaps the most obvious reason for this is because we are all exposed to different types of stressors. Nevertheless, even in cases where two people experience similar adverse experiences, how they make meaning of them won't be the same.

Why is this important?

Codependency is a relationship dynamic that only some people form. It isn't necessarily true that growing up in an abusive household or suffering with a mental health condition will make you codependent on others. Therefore, the likelihood of developing codependency or not has more to do with each unique individual, and how they cope with stressful events, and make meaning of their life experiences.

The remainder of the chapter will explore various risk factors of codependency. There is sufficient research to prove that these factors can make you more vulnerable to developing codependent behaviors. However, once again, being vulnerable to codependent behaviors doesn't mean that you will end up adopting this kind of dynamic with others.

Consider each risk factor and think about how they may have played a role (or continue to play a role) in your life.

Trauma and Codependency

Trauma is defined by the American Psychological Association (APA) as an emotional response to a painful life event (APA, 2021). Your body's reaction to trauma is to activate the stress response, also known as fight-flight-freeze mode.

Immediately after the traumatic event, depending on the circumstances, it is common to either become emotionally reactive (e.g. having anger episodes), withdraw from others and enter isolation, or go into a state of shock and denial.

The long-term effects of not getting into a therapy room and addressing the trauma immediately afterward, is the devastating impact on your mental health. How trauma affects your mental health may vary, but some of the common side effects include developing an anxiety disorder, depression, post-traumatic stress disorder (PTSD), or low self-esteem.

Early detection of these mental health conditions, and following a treatment plan, can reverse whatever emotional damage that may have started forming. However, the frightening reality is that many people don't seek help, but instead continue with life as normal.

Take a moment to imagine what "life as normal" might look like for someone who has unaddressed trauma. Would they *really* be able to continue as though nothing happened? It is highly unlikely. Depending on what kinds of traumatic events they were exposed to, various aspects of their life could change. This might include the collapse of their stable belief systems, to be replaced by fear-based beliefs. Or the lack of secure attachments to people, which would lead to unhealthy relationships.

For example, someone who experiences childhood trauma, particularly growing up with absent or abusive parents, may struggle with closeness when they are older. Even how they look at relationships might change, and instead of seeking mutual respect, support, and affection, they might seek validation. Anyone who can give them the attention they were deprived of as a child could be considered "the one," regardless of other relationship qualities they may be lacking.

This is how codependent relationships form. Two people who have lost sense of, or have never experienced healthy and secure relationships, create a trauma-bond as a way to cope with unresolved pain from previous life experiences. They find comfort in each other because they are familiar with dysfunctional relationships, and the various coping mechanisms that highly stressed individuals adopt to protect themselves, like people-pleasing, using manipulation tactics, or having porous boundaries.

The lingering trauma within codependent relationships doesn't mean that there is a lack of love. Just like any couple or parent-child relationship, there is a positive attraction or connection felt by both individuals. However, being in love doesn't make the parties any less vulnerable to being abused. In fact, the idea of "being in love" may in some cases make it difficult to address harmful behaviors or violations of boundaries.

Getting Behind the Trauma Bond

The term *trauma bond* was coined by Patrick Carnes, in 1997. He described it as an adaptive, dysfunctional attachment that emerges in the presence of shame, a perceived threat, or exploitation in order to survive (Lancer, 2022).

The bond is characterized by a power imbalance between the abuser and the one being abused. What attracts them to each other is surviving a history of trauma, but there is not much depth to their connection apart from that. The abuser is the dominant partner, who finds ways to belittle, manipulate, or control the other person. One of their favorite tactics is to play on the other person's fears and insecurities, like making an empty threat to leave the relationship whenever they are not getting their needs met.

Of course, the trauma bond doesn't start out abusive, and neither does the abuser make their intentions to seek control known in the beginning. At most, the relationship might feel unstable and unpredictable, with a mix of good and bad days. Over time, bad behavior becomes normalized, but at this point, the one being abused has accepted the status quo of their relationship.

Moreover, the pattern of abuse is typically followed by a pattern of intermittent positive reinforcement, which "trains" the person being abused to accept rewards after enduring abusive behavior. An example of this would be the abuser being extra affectionate and generous following their abuse. This creates a neediness in the other person, to always chase an elusive fairy tale of what their relationship could be, even though it is evident that the abuse will not end.

Research has shown that intermittent positive reinforcement conditions the brain to seek rewards, even when the rewards stop coming. This can explain why severing the trauma bond is so difficult. Even though the relationship is full of mostly lows, the potential of the relationship becomes an addiction. The hope of feeling loved by the abuser feels just as strong as if that love was actually there.

Givers can be vulnerable to creating trauma bonds. Their loyalty and incessant need for closeness is what causes them to keep seeking to win back the love of the taker. The more they lean toward the taker, the faster the taker runs in the other direction. But before the giver loses complete hope, the taker returns to offer them a taste of what genuine devotion feels like. This temporary display of affection is enough motivation to keep the giver chasing after the taker, not realizing that the cycle of detachment and reconnection will continue again.

Mental Illness and Codependency

Codependency is not a recognized mental illness, although it is seen as a condition sharing similarities with other personality disorders, like dependent personality disorder (DPD), post-traumatic stress disorder (PTSD), and borderline personality disorder (BPD).

Some of the mental health challenges that are linked with codependency include:

- stress
- anxiety
- depression
- low self-esteem
- emotional reactivity

The absence of a medical diagnostic criteria means that people who suffer with this condition are normally diagnosed with DPD instead, even though codependency isn't the same as DPD. The first for this being this way is the nature of relationships formed under the two conditions. Codependency, for instance, is characterized by dependent behavior focused on a specific individual, unlike DPD that is characterized by dependent behavior displayed to anyone in general.

The second reason why the two conditions aren't the same has to do with how the parties inside these relationship dynamics interact with each other. With DPD, there isn't always an enabler (i.e. the taker). There could simply be one person, the giver, who feels compelled to take care of their parent, child, friend, or loved one. Furthermore, this dynamic isn't always abusive. There can exist interdependence in the relationship, but the dependent person may feel anxious about being separated from their partner, or have doubts about taking care of themselves.

In contrast, a giver in a codependent relationship may show extreme devotion to the taker, to the extent of neglecting other responsibilities or relationships. Their identity and sense of self-worth revolves around the taker, and because the taker won't refuse the engulfing affection, the cycle of codependency continues.

Being In a Relationship With a Mentally Ill Person

Another way that codependency can develop is when one person in the relationship suffers with a mental illness. For instance, a child who takes care of their mentally ill parent may eventually take over their responsibilities, or a spouse who struggles with alcohol problems may need a lot of support and motivation from their family.

What makes it difficult to identify codependent behaviors when caring for a mentally ill loved one is because there is a natural attachment formed between you. You desire to express affection or seek validation from the ones you care about the most, and this makes it harder to know when you are extending yourself too much.

Even in healthy relationships, caretaking is seen as a form of love, and in some cases, an unavoidable task. For example, if your partner had depression and struggled to get themselves out of bed, most of the household responsibilities would fall on you. It isn't so much that they don't want to help you perform tasks around the house, it is that they physically cannot.

The only difference between caretaking in healthy relationships and codependent relationships is that there are clear boundaries enforced in the former. Whenever one person has reached the point of exhaustion from fulfilling the other's caretaking needs, they express a boundary. This can be as simple as saying "no."

The giver in a codependent relationship doesn't feel like enforcing boundaries is an option. They feel responsible for making sure their partner is happy and cared for, at all times. When they are unable to respond to their partner's needs, perhaps due to exhaustion, they may feel a sense of personal inadequacy. "How can I be so selfish?" they might think. Essentially, there are no limits to the amount of caretaking a giver can perform, which is what causes the power imbalance in their relationships.

Attachment and Codependency

John Bowlby's attachment theory explains the parent-child bond (referred to as an attachment), which starts forming inside the womb, but becomes noticeable when a child is about six weeks old (Cherry, 2022). By then, the child is able to show a preference for primary and secondary caregivers, and as the months go by, they develop a strong attachment to a specific caregiver (in most cases their birth mother).

The reason behind a child forming an attachment is that without the nurturing of other human beings, their physical and emotional survival would be on the line. They are quite literally dependent on their caregivers to create environments of safety and nourishment to avoid feelings of stress and anxiety.

When a child shows physical signs of distress, like crying, they are signaling for their caregiver's attention. They could be tired, hungry, or frightened, and desire for their parents to help them stabilize their nervous system and fulfill their needs. The close proximity to their caregiver, and knowing that their physical and emotional needs matter, is what develops a sense of security in the child, and makes exploring their identity and the world around them feel safe.

A caregiver who is absent (whether physically or emotionally) and misses several opportunities to respond to their child's needs, is seen to the child as someone who is unreliable. Without the security of a present and responsive caregiver, the child feels compelled to suppress their needs or look for other ways to get their caregiver's attention. This is what makes them vulnerable to developing codependency issues later on in life, and believing that their sense of self-worth is tied to the amount of validation they can receive from others.

Before we go into the discussion about the different attachment styles, grab a pen and write down responses to the following questions:

1. Can you remember the earliest memory being held by your parents? What did that experience feel like?

2. How would you describe the bond between you and your primary caregiver (the person who spent the most time taking care of you)?

3. Looking back to your early childhood, do you believe that your safety and affection needs were met?

4. Try to visualize your five-year-old self. What did that little boy or girl need to feel protected and cared for?

5. Based on the relationship with your primary caregiver, what kind of child were you? For example, were you extroverted, withdrawn, untrusting, temperamental, or confident?

Anxious Attachment

It is possible that you learned codependency as a result of how you were raised. Your physical and emotional needs may have been neglected, or fulfilled on random occasions, which taught you that love is conditional. Love felt like it had to be earned, rather than provided willingly.

The idea of love being conditional may have even led to harmful beliefs about intimacy and closeness with others. For example, you may have grown up believing that you needed to act a certain way to be accepted by others. Or being yourself and unapologetically expressing your needs may have felt unsafe, due to your caregivers dismissing your emotions, or overriding your right to choose how to experience reality.

Your early childhood ideas and beliefs about intimacy and closeness can be traced back to the type of attachment you formed with your primary caregiver, and reflected in your intimate adult relationships. Out of the four attachment styles outlined by the attachment theory, anxious attachment best describes how your codependent issues may have come from.

Anxious attachment develops during childhood as a response to inconsistent parenting. This means that your primary caregiver may have been physically present, but couldn't always recognize or respond promptly to your needs. Overtime, the patterns of inconsistent parenting created a strong need for your caregiver's affection, as well as a fear of losing or being separated from them.

A common behavior of a child with anxious attachment is crying uncontrollably whenever their primary caregiver leaves, like when the parents go to work or drop the kid off at daycare. While feeling nervous about being left alone is normal for most kids, it feels like abandonment for a child with anxious attachment.

Other common behaviors that are typical to inconsistent parenting are attention-seeking behaviors, like being completely silent, throwing tantrums, deliberately behaving badly, or being excessively clingy. The inconsistency can also cause confusion about what to expect from the caregiver in the future. As a result, the parent-child relationship can feel unpredictable and the child may struggle to feel comfortable in the presence of their parents.

Anxious attachment can follow you into adulthood and affect how you relate with others, particularly intimate partners. Since receiving love came with conditions when you were growing up, you may be drawn, or even seek out, people who are emotionally unavailable. As much as you try to avoid these types of lovers, the relationship dynamic feels familiar to you. Moreover, there is a part of you that believes you *can* earn the other person's love and inspire them—through your generous giving—to reciprocate your affection.

In exchange for responding to your partner's needs, you might desire for them to give you constant reassurance that they are not going to leave. When you are not given this reassurance, you may feel anxious, jealous, or suspicious of their motives. Remember, anxious attachment causes a fear of abandonment, and perhaps the worst thing that an intimate partner could do isn't necessarily treat you badly, but instead decide to seek affection from someone else, or end the relationship altogether.

The question about whether your partner loves you might constantly run through your mind, making you more vigilant for any signs of rejection. When you notice them becoming distant, for reasons unrelated to you (e.g. increased workload, personal family issues, or working on personal goals), your response may be to lean in, and dedicate more of your time and energy serving them. It is also normal for childhood attention-seeking behaviors to come up, which can create conflict in your relationship.

Addressing anxious attachment requires different kinds of interventions, many of which we will discuss later on in this book. However, for now, you can practice recognizing and accepting uncomfortable emotions that may be triggered by perceived disregard, avoidance, or rejection.

Emotions are messengers that arise inside your body to communicate how you are feeling about a particular experience. They are neither good nor bad, but instead show up to help you interpret what you are sensing. Whenever you sense a strong emotion arising, practice taking a powerful pause. Stop what you are doing and be still. Interrupt any thought that might cause your emotion to grow even stronger. Simply whisper to yourself, "not right now."

End the powerful pause when you feel calm, then begin to interpret your emotional experience. With curiosity, reflect on what you felt and put a name on it. For instance, was the emotion anger? If so, how could you tell? Did you feel your chest tightening or heart racing? Did you have an urge to yell or hurt your partner in some way?

Go a step further and think about what message the emotion came to deliver. In other words, based on the context of the situation, how come you felt angry? What happened that might have triggered this specific emotion? When you have gathered enough insight, complete the following sentence:

I feel [emotion] because [the reason behind the emotional trigger]. For example:

- I feel angry because my partner spoke to me in a way that felt unloving.
- I feel disregarded because I spent the night cooking for my mother, and she didn't show any appreciation.

- I feel embarrassed because I expressed a need to my friend, and they shut me down.

Recognizing and accepting your emotions may not heal your anxious attachment; however, it can help you learn how to be compassionate and responsive to your own needs.

Dysfunctional Families and Codependency

There is no such thing as a picture-perfect family. By nature, families fight as much as they fiercely love and protect each other. Parents and children will clash, and sometimes go days without speaking to one another. But that is how intimate relationships tend to be.

With that being said, there are some families that are dysfunctional, meaning that one or a few members within the family behave in ways that negatively impact the well-being of others. Some of the problems that might cause the dysfunctional dynamic include joblessness, depression, addictions, or personality disorders.

To better understand what dysfunctional families look like, we can compare them to how functional families are arranged. The table below provides common differences.

Functional Family	Dysfunctional Family
Enjoy spending time together, despite being of different ages and having different responsibilities.	Feel uncomfortable in family members' company, and tend to live separate lives.
Both parents and children honor rules and boundaries, but at times are willing to negotiate.	There are no clear rules and boundaries between parents and children, or that hold each family member accountable for their actions.
Parent-child bonds are built on mutual respect and acceptance of individual preferences.	Parents tend to show favoritism amongst children (i.e. the smartest or most agreeable child gets preferential treatment), or present respect as something that children need to earn.
Children receive unlimited and unconditional affection, and are raised in a safe environment where they can just be kids.	Children may feel unloved or neglected due to their parents' invalidating or harmful behaviors. Some children may also take on adult responsibilities at a young age, or be exposed to traumatic situations.
Family members are given the space to disagree with each other and have their own opinions, without feeling judged or intimidated.	Family members fear expressing their thoughts and feelings out of fear of upsetting one or few family members, which may lead to conflict.

Being raised in a dysfunctional family can make you vulnerable to developing codependency issues. The reason for this is that you were deprived of the one thing that every child deserves—emotional validation. The inability to receive empathy or unconditional love from your parents may have created an insatiable need to be accepted or feel wanted by others.

The lack of emotional validation also could have taught you to hide your needs and emotions. Back then, this may have been the only way to cope with feeling dismissed, criticized, or neglected by your parents. In adult relationships, the same behavior can cause you to attract abusive people, who continue to make you feel dismissed, criticized, and neglected.

What makes codependency seem "normal" to someone who grew up in a dysfunctional family is the fact that they were conditioned to accept unhealthy patterns of bonding and affection as being the standard behavior. For example, someone who wasn't allowed to voice their concerns or share opposing views, will most likely grow up to become someone who finds it difficult to assert boundaries with others. It isn't because they don't see the need for boundaries, but rather they weren't taught that asserting boundaries is okay.

Another example is someone who was raised in a dysfunctional family where anybody who wasn't a family member was seen as an outsider, and met with suspicion. They may have been taught to conceal family secrets and never show any signs of disloyalty to the core family. In adult relationships, they may struggle to speak out against abusive or unfair treatment from others, as this may be considered being disloyal. Moreover, shutting out friends and family from the relationship can create an unhealthy dependency on their intimate partner.

Before we move on to discussing different roles in a dysfunctional family, grab a pen and answer the following questions about your family:

1. Do you remember family members abusing drugs or alcohol growing up?

2. Were you raised by a parent who suffered from a mental illness?

3. Was it normal for family members to go for long periods of time without speaking to each other?

4. Was it normal for family members to yell, insult, mock, or physically attack each other?

5. Were there secrets in your household that were kept hidden from non-family members?

6. Were there some topics that were kept off limits in your household, such as mentioning negative emotions or bringing up a family member's abusive behavior?

7. Were you robbed of your childhood by assuming adult responsibilities at an early age?

8. Did many family conflicts revolve around one family member's dysfunctional behaviors?

9. Were one or more family members emotionally, physically, or sexually abusive?

10. Did you often dread seeing or being in the presence of one or more family members?

If you answered yes to one or more of these questions, it is likely that your codependency issues are, to some extent, a result of your family upbringing. This realization can be comforting because you at least know where you may have learned some of your behavioral patterns.

Six Dysfunctional Survival Roles

In order to cope in the dysfunctional environment and maintain relationships with each other, family members tend to adopt survival roles. You can think of survival roles as the substitute identities that each family member creates to preserve their sanity and prevent as much psychological harm to themselves as possible.

These survival roles can be adopted by parents and children; however, they have more negative long-term effects on children. It is also common for family members to adopt more than one role, or switch between roles whenever there are changes in the family. Nonetheless, the longer a substitute identity is maintained, the easier it is to integrate it to the real self, thereby causing semi-permanent personality and behavioral issues—including codependency.

Below are six types of survival roles you are likely to find within a dysfunctional family:

1. Addict

The addict can be a parent or child that develops a substance or behavioral addiction. This may be the best way they know how to cope with stress or difficult life changes. For example, after losing a job, the parent might develop a drinking problem as a way to cope with financial burdens. Or as a way to cope with being emotionally abused by their parent, the child may develop a food addiction.

The addict is oftentimes the one whom family conflict is centered around. Due to their addict behaviors, they may play the role of a victim or rebel. The constant turmoil they create within the family is fueled by their ongoing addiction.

2. Co-addict

The co-addict is usually the closest person to the addict. They might feel like they know the addict better than anyone else, and therefore enable most of their harmful behaviors. It is common for the co-addict to have codependency issues, since they seek approval and desire to "stay in the good books" of the addict.

When they are a parent, the co-addict can take the side of the addicted parent over the children. Their undying devotion to the addict is something they never want to be questioned, even when it means turning a blind eye to abusive behaviors. When the co-addict is a child, they might tolerate any kind of treatment from their addicted parent, despite the harm it may cause to them. They may even view their parent from an idealistic point of view, creating an almost godlike image that cannot be challenged.

3. Peacemaker

The peacemaker tends to suffer from chronic anxiety. They are on constant alert for any signs of conflict, and quick to find ways of defusing it. What's interesting about the peacemaker is that they aren't loyal to any particular family member, which allows them to observe family dynamics, various personality traits of members, and lead with empathy when seeking to resolve conflict.

Due to their calm and understanding approach, they are able to get through to the addict and the co-addict, and make them aware of the impact of their behaviors on other family members. Of course, this may not lead to changed behaviors, but it can cause temporary reconciliation.

The peacemaker is vulnerable to codependency issues because, as part of their caretaking responsibilities, they often prioritize the needs of others and suppress their own needs. Children who are peacemakers tend to become adults who subconsciously seek partners they can take care of, such as people with mental health or chronic physical illnesses. The desire to attempt to save others from experiencing the consequences of their actions is something that the peacemaker will find very difficult to switch off.

4. Golden child

The golden child is the one who is given preferential treatment by the addict. In the addict's eyes, this particular child can do no wrong. The reason why this child is chosen over the others is due to their desirable qualities. For instance, they may be born with a unique talent, look extremely beautiful, or show above average competence at school.

These are all qualities that the addict sees as reflections of their own desirability. In other words, the golden child is not praised because of how phenomenal they are, but because of how good they make their parent look.

The golden child grows up believing that they are only good when they are achieving something. As such, they may grow up to be perfectionists, people-pleasers, or adopt different personas depending on who they are around.

5. Mascot

The mascot is typically one of the younger kids in a family, who is born into an already dysfunctional environment. Similar to the peacemaker, they can also suffer from chronic anxiety; however, they deal with it by finding ways of making the atmosphere at home lighter.

For instance, they will always use humor to defuse a tense situation or distract themselves from confronting strong emotions. Every time they are able to make other family members laugh, they feel an even greater responsibility to provide humor during stressful situations. Consequently, they are never able to express their thoughts and feelings with others because of the clownish personality they have created.

Children who are mascots are likely to grow up as people-pleasers who calm the fears of others through humor or other light-hearted behaviors. This can easily put them in a caretaker role, where they can use their "clown skills" to make their loved ones feel comforted.

6. Lost child

The lost child copes with the dysfunction at home by isolating themselves from other family members, and taking care of their own needs as much as possible. They are most likely to be labeled as the "rebel" or "black sheep" of the family because of their deliberate refusal to play along with the unhealthy patterns of behaviors that exist.

A lost child may grow up to have self-esteem issues, see themselves as a victim, or look for people who can take care of them. Instead of attracting needy people, they are often the one who displays needy or clingy behaviors in adult relationships.

As mentioned above, the consequences of being part of a dysfunctional family are mostly felt by children. From the time they are born, children raised in these types of homes lose touch of what is normal and healthy. What is important for them is surviving the treacherous environment they are born into, and this leads to developing survival instincts that make them feel safe.

We have explored four risk factors that can make you vulnerable to developing codependency. These are trauma, mental illness, attachment issues, and being raised in a dysfunctional family. Once again, it is possible to have experienced any of these risk factors and not develop codependency issues. Nonetheless, it is still good to reflect and assess the role and impact of past experiences, including your childhood upbringing, on how you relate and form bonds with others.

3

Recognize How Codependency Looks In Different Relationships

"The child lacking a sense of welcome, joyous belonging, gratuitous security, will learn to hoard the limited supply of affection [...] When the gift of belonging with is denied, the child learns that love means belonging to."

— SAM KEEN

Recognizing Codependency in Different Relationships

Codependent relationships won't all look the same. In some relationships, the roles of giver and taker may not be so obvious, perhaps due to the nature of the relationship.

A good example would be the relationship between an employee and a manager. An employee signs a work contract to carry out certain tasks and responsibilities. It is perfectly acceptable for the manager to offer direction on how to complete these tasks and responsibilities,

RECOGNIZE HOW CODEPENDENCY LOOKS IN DIFFERENT RELATIONSHIPS

but when they are constantly looking over the employee's shoulder, redoing completed work, or being overly "helpful," they may start to micromanage.

If neither the employee nor manager know what the signs of codependency look like, they both might accept this controlling relationship as being normal. Think of a time when you felt like a powerless employee under the leadership of a dominant boss. Were you aware that you were part of a codependent relationship?

The following section will look at various real-life examples of codependent relationships, beyond the common romantic relationship. However, before we go into each example, it is important for you to learn the basic signs of codependency, as these are the red flags that show up early into any kind of relationship. These signs include:

- One person has the need to prove themselves to another.
- One person's self-worth is tied to how useful they can be to another.
- One person unconsciously apologizes constantly to another.
- One person decides to withhold their opinions to maintain peace in the relationship.
- One person has the tendency to avoid confrontation.
- One person has the tendency to ignore or downplay their own needs and desires.
- One person feels an excessive need to help, save, or fix another.
- One person feels guilty doing something for themselves.
- One person agrees to doing activities they don't enjoy to please another.
- One person experiences an overwhelming fear of rejection or abandonment.

While the context of your codependent relationship may be different, you will be able to notice a few of the signs mentioned above. When this happens, you have the opportunity to turn things around and restore a balanced power dynamic between you and the other person.

Codependency in Romantic Relationships

Two people enter a romantic relationship out of the desire to be together. The unspoken expectation is that both people will strive to respond to each other's needs. For as long as the couple continues to balance the amount of giving and taking, the relationship can remain mutually beneficial. But as soon as one person develops an over-reliance on their significant other, codependency issues can emerge.

The common myth about codependency in romantic relationships is that someone who is independent cannot develop codependency issues. The underlying belief behind this myth is that being self-sufficient prevents neediness.

The truth, however, is that independent people can find themselves entangled in codependent relationships. They may be completely self-sufficient, but have an unhealthy desire to be needed by others. This unhealthy desire is what attracts an independent person to a needy and clingy individual, who doesn't mind giving them the validation and sense of control they seek.

Another common myth about codependency in romantic relationships is that developing this type of dynamic is a choice. In the past, you may have listened to people say to you, "Stop trying to rescue people!" or "Why do you care about someone who obviously doesn't care about you?" These kinds of sentiments imply that you have a choice in the

RECOGNIZE HOW CODEPENDENCY LOOKS IN DIFFERENT RELATIONSHIPS

matter, as though you can flick a switch and eliminate your caretaking tendencies.

However, the relationship between a giver and taker is far more complicated than that. The act of taking care of others to the point of sacrificing their own needs is not something the giver is conscious of most of the time. But even when they do notice the power imbalance in their relationship, it is something that brings much anxiety and shame, rather than changed behavior.

For many givers, the need to take care of others began at a young age, before they were even aware that they were behaving in that manner. It was a coping mechanism to deal with stress and maintain relationships with loved ones. In other words, caretaking was a survival instinct that made the giver feel safe, and provided a false illusion of being loved and accepted by their caregivers. The more they self-sacrificed, the better they felt about themselves.

This is why caretaking in codependent romantic relationships isn't much of a choice. Even in adult relationships, it is still a viable coping mechanism to deal with stress and feel some kind of connection to one's significant other. The giver's sense of self-worth is linked to how much love they can earn. Therefore, there are no limits to how much they can do for the man or woman they love.

Lastly, there is a difference in codependent romantic relationships between helping and enabling your significant other. Helping your partner generally refers to offering assistance or support. When they are upset, for example, you may offer to listen and empathize with what they are going through. The aim is to empower them to get out of the rut, so they can find a solution to their problem.

Enabling strives to keep your partner depended on your care and support. Instead of empowering them to solve their own problem, you create dependency by solving the problem for them, helping them avoid consequences, or telling them what they want to hear. As a result, your partner may learn to seek help from you whenever they find themselves in trouble, rather than relying on their own skills, insight, and experience to overcome challenges.

Based on the explanation offered above, here are a few real-life scenarios of what codependency looks like in romantic relationships:

Over-compromising

Tanya's partner expresses that they want to see more of her. This request comes after a conversation about her busy work schedule. During the conversation, she mentions how work is going to demand a lot more of her time because she is working on exciting career goals.

Unfortunately, her partner is less than excited to hear about the news, since it means that he won't get to spend as much time with her.

Out of fear of jeopardizing her relationship, Tanya makes an agreement to spend two nights out of the week at her partner's place. This compromise doesn't seem to satisfy him, citing that he feels like he is competing with her work.

To avoid further conflict about this issue, Tanya agrees to spend four nights out of the week at his place. This arrangement seems to be enough to get him off her back, but it also means that Tanya isn't able to devote as much time to her career goals as she had planned.

Dependency on their advice

Pete struggles to make up his mind when making decisions and often goes to his partner for advice on what to do. Every choice, whether small or large, gets approved by his partner before he can take action.

At the beginning of their relationship, this was quite a turn on. He loved the idea of his partner having so much of a say about important matters in his life. However, after some time, this feeling has been replaced with the fear of not getting his partner's approval on important decisions.

For example, their "no" feels ten times worse than any kind of rejection. It doesn't matter how excited Pete was about the plan, hearing "no" from his partner is enough to cancel whatever idea he had in mind.

Moreover, when his partner expresses disapproval about someone, like Pete's friend or family member, he regards their opinion as the truth, and assumes the same negative attitude toward their loved one. In Pete's eyes, his partner knows better than him, and is more capable of making good decisions on Pete's behalf.

Desire to be needed

Brandon enjoys playing the provider role in his romantic relationship. As such, he tends to attract women who desire to be financially taken care of. This doesn't bother Brandon like it would other people because he finds pleasure in being depended upon. Sometimes, he goes as far as setting restrictions on how much money to give his girlfriend, asking for receipts as proof of their purchases, or creating rules on how they are supposed to spend their money.

For as long as his girlfriend remains reliant on his financial allowances, Brandon maintains the upper hand in the relationship. He feels a sense of self-worth for being able to take care of his significant other, and less fearful about the possibility of his girlfriend leaving him.

Codependency in Parent-Child Relationships

Besides romantic relationships, codependency can also appear in parent-child relationships. Typically, the primary caregiver (in most cases, the mother) will form an unhealthy attachment with their child, to the extent of controlling the child's life. To outsiders, this parent-child attachment may seem normal and loving, but behind closed doors, the parent may be either overly-reliant or exert dominance over their child.

Since codependency in parent-child relationships can be so subtle, below are a few tell-tale signs to look out for:

- **Parent holds too much control.** The parent's self-worth thrives on their child's neediness. They seek to take away as much autonomy as possible from their child to keep them in a state of constantly seeking their physical, emotional, or financial support.
- **Parent does not respect boundaries.** The parent views their child as an extension of themselves, therefore they don't see a need to respect their child's boundaries. They may be overly invested in their child's private life, stalk them on social media, share their child's personal secrets with others, or refuse to take their child's "no" seriously.
- **Parent sacrifices other relationships to care for their child.** The parent may devote 24 hours, 7 days a week, to spending time and nurturing their child. Consequently, other relationships

with friends and family may fall away. It is also common for the codependent parent to be a single mother or father, or have a strained relationship with their romantic partner.

- **Parent manipulates their child's emotions.** Due to the desire for control, the parent learns various tactics to get their child to behave exactly how they want. Instead of using aggressive strategies, like yelling or name-calling, which may not always get the child to act accordingly, the parent may learn passive-aggressive strategies, like using the silent treatment, projecting their feelings, stirring up guilt.
- **Parent believes that they are always right.** The parent finds it difficult to recognize when they are in the wrong and apologize for their mistakes. In their world, they are always right, and may feel personally attacked when confronted about their harmful behaviors.
- **Parent fears disciplining their child.** Due to the fear of rejection, the codependent parent fears setting boundaries with their child and correcting bad behavior. They would much rather prefer overlooking disrespect and preserving a good relationship with their child than enforcing discipline and risk being disliked by their child.

Codependency in parent-child relationships can lead to emotional abuse. The child may feel unsafe to express their genuine thoughts and feelings, which causes them to comply to the needs of their parent. When they reach adolescence, they may find it difficult to develop their own identity separate from their parent, or may feel uncertain about gaining independence, speaking up for themselves, or imagining a life where they don't need their parent's assistance.

Please note that codependent parents are not necessarily abusive;

however, the excessive need for control can, in some cases, trigger personality disorders like NPD or BPD. For example, a codependent parent becomes manipulative when they play the victim in order to make their child feel guilty or lure them into taking care of them. Alternatively, a codependent parent displays narcissistic traits when they value their own feelings and comfort above their child's, and only seek control to keep the child in a submissive position.

Based on the explanation offered above, here are a few real-life scenarios of what codependency looks like in parent-child relationships:

Extreme focus on the child

Suzanne's world revolves around the safety of her child. Due to her own tumultuous upbringing, she is committed to providing her child with the utmost affection. She monitors several cameras around the house to track her child's movements. To rule out illnesses, her child's body temperature is kept at a specific level, and all inflammation-causing foods are banned from their home—including sugary treats like soda, candy, and chocolates.

As part of keeping her child safe, Suzanne has also implemented certain rules regarding who has access to her child, and how much time they spend with them. When her child is unhappy, she feels personally responsible for their moods. Her sole task in those moments is to give her child whatever they need to make them happy again. At times, Suzanne is unable to cheer her child up, and this makes her feel like an incompetent parent.

Guilt-tripping

Divina often shares her painful childhood memories with her child. She feels as though people from her past were never held accountable for the wrong committed against her. Having a child has been Divina's way of finally getting somebody to pay for the wrongdoings of those in her past. She expects her child to provide the care that wasn't given to her as a little girl.

Divina's child is too young to understand her mother's complex needs, and how to respond to them in the exact manner she likes. At times, her child rebels and attempts to draw a boundary. However, Divina quickly pulls out the victim card to garner sympathy. The end goal is to get her child to perform the various caretaking duties that are required. When her child complies, they are rewarded with positive reinforcement, like being given a hug or told how much they are loved.

Being overly emotional

Jaden doesn't respond well when her child refuses to do what she says—which in her mind is seen as a sign of disrespect. Instead of expressing how she feels and giving her child an opportunity to respond, Jaden becomes emotional.

Sometimes, she might yell and make verbal threats. Other times, she uses the silent treatment and withholding affection to show her disapproval. Whenever it seems like she is losing an argument, she tends to divert attention away from herself and recall a painful past experience that makes her cry hysterically.

All of these displays of emotion make it difficult for Jaden to listen during arguments and empathize with her child. Without properly listening, she can make the wrong assumptions about her child's intentions, like accusing them of being insensitive or spiteful. What's important to her at those moments is how uncomfortable, disrespected, or unloved she feels.

Codependency in Friendships

It takes more than shared interests to make a friendship work. Like any relationship, there must be a good balance of give and take. A friendship where one person is doing most of the communicating, organizing, or supporting can create codependency.

One of the ways of keeping a friendship healthy is to establish solid boundaries. These boundaries are what protect both parties' needs, values, and interests from being taken for granted. When there aren't clear boundaries between friends, the two can become enmeshed in one another, and lose their sense of individuality.

Enmeshment won't always feel like you are being suffocated by your friend. At times, it can be as subtle as thinking and feeling the same way as them. This should raise alarm bells, especially if you remember having unique opinions, beliefs, and goals before you started getting close with your friend. The mark of true friendship isn't about finding your "twin" or "better half" who can finish your sentences and physically feel your distress. True friendship is about creating a safe space where two unique individuals can express who they are and feel supported.

Besides a lack of boundaries, codependent friendships create a power imbalance, where one friend does most of the giving, and the other does most of the taking. Below are a few signs of codependency in friendships:

- **One friend seeks constant reassurance.** This friend might need excessive amounts of support through long phone calls, chronic texting, or asking for your advice on a number of different life circumstances. When there are brief moments of silence, they may suspect that something is wrong in your friendship.
- **One friend spends too much time fixing the other's problems.** Giving solicited and unsolicited advice can become a habit, especially for a friend who enjoys feeling needed by others. They will invest a lot of time and energy in analyzing their friend's problem, and offering solutions—even though they may have unresolved issues of their own.
- **When one person is upset, the other feels upset, too.** Codependent friends often share emotions because of how few boundaries they have around their emotional lives. After some time, their moods can be dictated by how the other person is feeling.
- **One friend feels energized, while the other feels drained after spending time together.** The taker tends to lean on their giver friend for emotional support. In true giver style, they will expend all of their time and energy to make sure their friend leaves feeling lighter and happier. The same supportive environment is not created for the giver, which often means they walk away feeling emotionally exhausted.
- **One or both friends relies significantly on the survival of the friendship.** Codependent friends don't typically have many other friends outside their relationship. They heavily rely on each other to fulfill a heap of needs. Both the giver and taker in the dynamic get something out of the friendship, which perpetuates the cycle of codependency.

Codependency in friendships tends to be glamorized and seen as a measure of how much the friends love each other. The truth, however, is that codependency creates an obsession with the other person, not a genuine affection toward them. It is seeing your friend as an object that you can use to satisfy your emotional needs, and not a human being who has unique desires and outlook on life.

There isn't any real respect and connection between codependent friends, even though it may feel like it. What keeps the friendship going is the transactional power dynamic, where both the giver and taker get something out of being friends with each other. When the codependent friendship ends, it is common to have doubts about whether the friendship was real in the first place—or if it was simply the result of one person being needy and the other person desiring to be needed.

Based on the explanation offered above, here are a few real-life scenarios of what codependency looks like in friendships:

Feeling emotionally drained

Hannah's friendship with Buella consumes most of her time and energy. During the week, the two of them text constantly throughout the day, and every weekend is spent together.

Over time, Hannah has noticed that her friend relies significantly on her for emotional support. Whenever she struggles to get out of bed, resolve conflict with her boyfriend, or deal with everyday stress, Buella's first instinct is to call Hannah.

Hannah feels guilty for needing time away from Buella, even though she knows that it will be good for her mental health. Since the friendship began, her needs have taken a back seat because of the amount of problems constantly arising in Buella's life that require Hannah's undivided attention. Nevertheless, she knows that if she continues to give unconditional support, she will soon reach the point of emotional burnout.

Support from one direction

TJ has always been an attentive friend, who intuitively knows how to respond to his friends' needs. He has built a reputation for saving his friends from the most outrageous situations, and making sure that they are taken care of. However, over the past few years, he has noticed that whenever he needs help, his friends are unavailable.

The first few times weren't a big deal. He was low on cash and needed a favor from close friends, who all politely declined. On another occasion, TJ asked one of his best buddies to fetch him from the airport the following week, but once again they were unable to assist him.

The most recent time, TJ was struggling with a difficult coworker and needed someone to vent to. He tried calling a few of his close friends, but only one picked up his call. When he began speaking, his friend found ways of turning the conversation to him, explaining a recent fight with a coworker. TJ never got the opportunity to open up and share his feelings. Instead, he ended up giving his friend advice on how to resolve the conflict with his coworker.

Jealousy over other relationships

Indigo and Sam are best friends. They work similar jobs, live in the same neighborhood, and enjoy the same social activities. Recently, Sam got into a romantic relationship. At first, Indigo seemed supportive, but after some time, she expressed feeling left out.

For the first time, Indigo doesn't get to see or talk to Sam every day. This adjustment hasn't been easy, since she depended on her friend for validation. Now that they hardly get to see each other, Indigo feels inadequate as a friend. She is upset with Sam for seemingly abandoning her, but also secretly yearns for the same bond Sam shares with her boyfriend.

As the giver, Sam tries to spend equal amounts of time with her best friend and boyfriend, but doesn't get it right all the time. She feels guilty, knowing that Indigo is having a hard time adjusting, and attempts to show her in different ways that their friendship will remain unchanged. What she doesn't realize is that the only thing that would satisfy Indigo is if Sam were single again, so she could have her undivided attention.

Codependency in Work Relationships

Codependency issues exist at work, as much as they do at home. Codependent workers step into a workplace and quickly make it their own. They feel personally responsible for achieving the mission of the company, or turning their department into a success.

On the surface, this seems great. After all, employees who are passionate and self-driven are every employer's dream. Unlike other employees, codependent workers don't need to be pushed or supervised to perform their job. They are typically high-performers and will deliver exceptional results from day one.

To get ahead in the company, codependent workers will go as far as studying their coworkers, from colleagues within their team to senior managers on an executive level. They want to know who does what, and how to appeal to each individual's needs.

Codependent workers will sacrifice their own personal time and energy to impress coworkers and develop good relationships with others. If they aren't careful, they can become overworked and burned out. However, to them, this is a small price to pay to stay on others' good books and advance in their career.

The ugly side of a codependent worker's personality is that they can be controlling. This controlling nature is often seen when things don't go their way. Remember that codependent people seek control from external sources to feel good about themselves. When they are not in a powerful position, they can feel insecure. Even if they are not the person in charge, it is common for the codependent worker to display leadership traits. They feel responsible for supervising their team members and making sure work tasks are carried out in a certain manner.

When their suggestions are not taken, the codependent worker can feel resentful, and find passive-aggressive ways of showing their annoyance. For instance, they might not share information that can assist team members in doing their job (a form of subtle sabotage), or they might privately complain to management about their fellow coworker.

Another explosive trait of a codependent worker is their emotional meltdowns at work. Due to the amount of responsibility they carry upon their shoulders, and the fear of sharing and releasing strong emotions, the codependent worker can experience frequent meltdowns. When they are overwhelmed, they can cry, yell, or criticize others. Since they do such a good job of covering up their frustrations, these meltdowns can seem like they came out of nowhere.

Most times, meltdowns are signs that the codependent worker needs a break. They may have been working tireless hours on a stressful project, managing difficult employees, and neglecting their own physical and mental well-being to produce quality results for the company.

Based on the explanation offered above, here are a few real-life scenarios of what codependency looks like at work:

Obsessive need for control

Joe manages a team of 20 employees. His sense of self is enhanced by the people he works with on a daily basis. Although the team is highly skilled and experienced at what they do, Joe feels the need to constantly watch over them, provide instructions, and assess progress on a weekly basis.

No detail or task performed by team members gets approved without Joe's input. Most times, he will scrutinize the work produced and offer suggestions to improve it. Employees sometimes feel discouraged when their quality work is sent back for further improvements. They believe that Joe's performance standards may be impossible to reach.

Joe believes that he is helping the team by teaching them how to pursue excellence. He was raised by parents who demanded a lot out of him as a child, which led him to become a high achiever. He envisions leading a team of high achievers, who are capable of delivering work that meets his level of satisfaction.

Friend and foe

Selena is a people's person and enjoys networking at work. She can strike up a conversation with anyone, and walk away having made a new friend. Her social skills have enabled her to gain the trust of several coworkers, including her manager and the top boss.

However, Selena has a secret. She isn't the fun, bubbly, and agreeable person that everyone has come to love. In fact, this persona is strictly put on for work purposes.

Behind the mask, Selena is highly critical of others and seeks to have the upper hand in every relationship. Over the years, she has studied human behavior and learned how to interact with different types of people, in a personal and professional environment.

Instead of openly disagreeing with others, she will find discrete ways of venting her frustrations. For instance, she might complain about one coworker to another, play the role of victim to gain sympathy, or use her close proximity to management to influence certain rules and policies at work.

Whenever Selena is accused of doing any of these things, she experiences an emotional breakdown. She fears being disliked or rejected by others, and therefore must have coworkers on her side at all times. Being emotional is her way of deflecting from her questionable behaviors and releasing the anxiety of being found out.

Self-sacrificing

Dorothy is a self-driven "boss babe," who is passionate about her job. However, she sets incredibly high expectations for herself to accomplish exceptional results, all the time!

In the office, she is the first in and last out, but continues to work even at home. Her work day doesn't really have a set start and end time because of the excessive amount of work she willingly takes on.

Dorothy makes it a point to tell others how busy she is. Part of the satisfaction of working hard is getting praise and recognition for her contribution. She feels compelled to share with others how great of a sacrifice she is making by working extra hours and missing out on personal commitments. When she isn't given the attention she wants, she may pout, complain, or play the victim.

It is easy for Dorothy to feel taken for granted by her coworkers when they don't acknowledge her sacrifices. What her coworkers don't realize is that all of her giving is done in exchange for constant validation. For as long as she feels seen and appreciated, she will go above and beyond for them—to the detriment of her own well-being.

Exercises to Become a Better Version of You

Healing codependent relationships is a lengthy process that requires several kinds of interventions, many of which will be outlined in the book. However, to support these interventions, you must start by empowering yourself!

At the end of the day, strategies are just strategies. What makes them effective isn't the step-by-step process, but the person who chooses to implement them. You are the x-factor that makes healing from codependency possible. When you are determined to heal your relationships, you give the various strategies new life.

Below are two exercises to become a better version of yourself within current relationships. Continuously practicing these exercises will open your mind to new ways of relating to yourself and others.

Exercise 1: Recognize and Express Your Needs

Perhaps when you were a child, you didn't feel safe sharing your thoughts and feelings with others, so instead you taught yourself how to deny or minimize your needs. Alternatively, you may have been raised by parents who made you feel inferior to them and constantly criticized or downplayed your needs.

In adult relationships, you can find yourself repeating the same parent-child dynamic; where you play the role of the invisible child and your partner plays the role of the overpowering parent.

To avoid this dynamic from repeating itself, it is important to remind yourself that having needs is not the same as being needy. The aim of adult relationships is to create a safe space where both parties take turns expressing and responding to each other's needs.

However, before you can feel empowered to express your needs, it is important to learn how to recognize what you need in the first place. The best way to recognize your needs is to acknowledge and embrace emotions. If this is an uncomfortable step for you, focus more on exploring what you feel than sitting with your emotions.

Bring your awareness to the physical sensations flowing throughout your body. Notice the parts of your body that feel light and tense. Focusing on your physical sensations can be a beginner-friendly way of teaching yourself to recognize comfortable and uncomfortable sensations. You can learn that comfortable body sensations, like calm breathing or relaxed muscles, make you feel light. In contrast, uncomfortable body sensation, like shortness of breath or stiff muscles, make you feel tense.

The next level is to associate physical comfort and discomfort with emotional messages. For example, when you experience a shortness of breath, what type of uncomfortable emotions might that sensation be signaling? Could it be signaling fear, anxiety, or nervousness? Or when you experience stomach pain, could it be signaling distress, sadness, or loneliness?

Continue to explore the various emotional messages that different physical sensations might be signaling. Write down your observations below. Note that there are no right or wrong answers.

_____
_____
_____
_____
_____

Once you are able to recognize what you are feeling, the next step is to reflect on why you feel that way. Determine what might have happened to signal that particular emotion. Instead of focusing on the recent situation that played out between you and the other person, think back to experiences that have shaped what you deem pleasurable and threatening.

Ask yourself what early childhood conditioning might be at play. Could this situation have triggered childhood fears and insecurities? Did the other person say a word or speak in a way that took you back to experiences? Or did their actions bring back fears of being rejected or abandoned?

Exploring your experiences will help you make sense of why you are feeling emotional, and where your emotions possibly stem from. The more comfortable you are interpreting past experiences, the easier it will be to track your emotions. As you explore, write down memories that come up and how they impacted you below.

Now that you have explored your emotions, you are ready to acknowledge and express your needs. All emotions stem from met and unmet needs. The feeling of calmness, for example, is proof that your need for emotional safety has been met. But feeling anxious, on the other hand, is proof that your need for emotional safety has not been met.

You can use pleasurable and unpleasurable emotions to identify met and unmet needs. Look at the list of emotions below and identify what met and unmet needs they reveal:

- sadness
- self-doubt
- happiness
- rejection
- feeling loved

When you are feeling strong emotions, recognize that you are suffering because of unmet needs. If your needs were being met, you would feel calm, open, and comfortable. You can think as far back as your childhood to identify unmet needs that could be triggered by present experiences. Once you are able to recognize the unmet need, the final step is to communicate it.

The best way to communicate unmet needs is to be clear and phrase your sentences in a way that makes your request easy to understand. Don't assume the other person can intuitively sense what you need, or how their behaviors may have affected you. You can follow the steps below to improve the way you articulate unmet needs.

To practice this short exercise, think about a common unmet need in any type of relationship (i.e. romantic, parent-child, social, or work relationship), then follow the steps.

- **Describe your observations**

Explain the pattern of behavior that you have picked up. Speak from your point of view, and try not to assume how the situation looks from the other person's side. Use "I" statements to state what you are noticing. E.g. I noticed that you don't acknowledge me when you come back from work.

- **Describe how you feel**

Let the other person know how you feel as a result of their actions. Once again, describe the emotional impact without making judgments or accusations. Use "I" statements to describe your experience. E.g. When you walk past me without greeting or giving me a kiss, I feel unimportant.

- **Be upfront about your needs**

This is your opportunity to express what you need from the other person. Remember that having needs is not the same as being needy. Someone who loves and respects you won't feel burdened by the idea of responding to your needs, especially when you do the same for them. Your needs matter to them because your happiness is what makes the relationship sweeter!

When stating your needs, be upfront. Describe in specific terms what you want them to start doing. E.g. I need you to acknowledge me when you get home by showing affection, like giving me a kiss or hug.

Exercise 2: Start Your Individuation Journey

If you were raised by a codependent parent, then it is possible that you skipped the individuation stage, which often begins in the teenage years. Individuation is the process of finding yourself, separate from your parent's identity. Think of it as a period of exploration where you grapple with different ideas about who you are, what you believe, and which direction you desire to go in life.

The process occurs naturally amongst adolescent children, but since codependent parents tend to be controlling, their children never get to discover who they are, or even form opinions that are unique from theirs.

Individuation has no age limits. It is a lifelong process that accommodates several personal transformations. Whenever you pick up a new life role or responsibility, you have the opportunity to continue the individuation process, and redefine who you are.

If you never undertook the individuation journey when you were younger, the good news is that you can start the process now! Psychiatrist Carl Jung presents five stages for undertaking the individuation journey. However, to prepare for this journey, he explains three aspects of your psyche which play a role in the process: the ego, persona, and shadow (Moulik, 2022).

The ego is the perception you have about who you are. It produces an identity (sense of "I") that makes you aware of being human. Your ego evolves over time, which means that the perceptions you hold about yourself are also likely to change.

The persona is the self-image created to showcase your identity. Unlike the ego, the persona is a mask that is worn to gain approval from others and feel a sense of belonging in a group or community. If you are lucky, your persona will reveal glimpses of who you are, but never the entirety of your being.

The shadow consists of the buried parts of who you are, which are seen as undesirable or unacceptable, according to society's standards. Many of your "dark" traits, like having a short-temper, being envious of others, or people-pleasing, are hidden in the shadow. Nonetheless, under significant stress, these repressed traits are triggered and reveal themselves through actions, attitudes, or dreams.

According to Carl Jung, these elements of the psyche exist in every human being. The challenge is to learn how to strike a good balance between them, so you can build a stable sense of self.

During the individuation journey, your ego, persona, and shadow will reveal themselves. You will get a chance to be acquainted with parts of you that are familiar, parts of you that come as a surprise, and also parts of you that are difficult to accept. Remember that both the acceptable and unacceptable parts of you make up the whole; you are neither completely good nor are you completely bad. You are a culmination of beliefs, mindsets, habits, and traits, which make you unique!

Consider the five stages of the individuation process, and answer the subsequent questions.

Stage 1: Suffering
One of the truths that Buddha taught was, "Life is suffering." By this he meant that in life, we will never be placed in perfect conditions.

There will always be good and bad times, which provide both pleasure and pain, thereby causing us to never feel fully satisfied.

The journey of finding who you are begins in a place of suffering because only pain, rather than pleasure, can lead to growth. When you go through difficult times, where your picture-perfect reality is threatened, you get to discover who you are, and what you are truly made of. However, you must choose to learn from your suffering instead of defining yourself by it, in order to self-actualize.

Below are a few questions to help you learn from past suffering:

- What difficult memory are you avoiding?

- What story, belief, or attitude is tied to this memory?

- How is this story, belief, or attitude impacting your life?

- What would happen if you continued to hold on to the story, belief, or attitude?

- What would happen if you chose to let go of the story, belief, or attitude?

- What pain do you need to let go of to make peace with this memory?

Stage 2: Integrating Your Shadow

Once you have acknowledged the parts of you that are in pain, the next step is to accept the traits and behaviors that have been repressed for many years. Any thought, emotion, or behavior that is seen as undesirable or unacceptable is thrown into the shadow, so that your self-image is only made up of what you believe others might approve of.

RECOGNIZE HOW CODEPENDENCY LOOKS IN DIFFERENT RELATIONSHIPS

If you grew up with a codependent parent, it is possible that some aspects of your personality or common childish behaviors were seen as unacceptable. Perhaps your parent didn't approve of you showing anger, being curious, embracing your sexuality, or having strong opinions. To avoid separation between you and your parent, you learned to hide these so-called undesirable parts of you in the shadow.

To fully heal from suffering, emotional wounds and unattended parts of you must be acknowledged and embraced as being a fundamental piece of your life story. You may not identify with some of those dark traits right now, but that doesn't mean that they cannot be brought to light and integrated into your psyche.

Integrating your shadow, also known as shadow work, is an act of self-acceptance (which we will explore in depth later on in the book). Instead of rejecting parts of you that were neglected as a child, you choose to act compassionately and embrace your imperfections.

Below are some questions to lovingly embrace your shadow:

- If you had to describe yourself to someone, which traits would you emphasize and which would you leave out?

- What are some of the family patterns you fear repeating in your adult life? How have these patterns shaped your life?

- In what situations do you feel less than others, equal to others, and better than others?

- What are some beliefs you have inherited from your parents? When were these beliefs introduced to you?

- Describe the earliest memory of feeling rejected by a loved one. What story or belief did you create after that moment?

- When was the last time you felt jealous of someone? What did they have that you wanted for yourself?

- How comfortable are you expressing anger? What are the overt or covert ways you show anger?

- Did you feel accepted for who you are as a child? How much of your true self did you feel comfortable showcasing to others?

- What emotions do you often avoid? How do you avoid them?

- Which aspect of yourself do you find most difficult to accept? What makes it so hard to accept?

Stage 3: Anima/Animus

So far, you have acknowledged past suffering and accepted repressed aspects of yourself. The third stage of individuation is to identify polarities, so you can embrace your "whole" self.

As a child, you may have been taught to be a "good girl" or "good boy," and given specific standards to uphold. However, authenticity is about being your genuine self, which consists of two polarities: anima and animus.

Jung describes the anima and animus as feminine and masculine energy that exists in each human being. Women tend to have more feminine energy than masculine energy, and men tend to have more masculine energy than feminine energy. Finding balance would therefore involve embracing the polar energy that is less active within.

Note that the energy you most resonate with doesn't have to be associated with your gender. For example, there are men who may have more feminine energy than masculine energy. They may feel comfortable around feminine qualities and expressions, and estranged from traditional masculine qualities and expressions. Finding balance for them would entail connecting more to the animus, masculine energy, since that is less active within.

Being fixed on one mode of being, such as embracing only feminine or masculine qualities, means that you constantly tap into the same part of you whenever you are confronted with new life circumstances. For instance, if you are a man, your default response to life might be to think logically, neglecting the emotional impact of the situation. As a woman, your default response to life might be to lead with passion, doing what feels right, rather than what makes logical sense.

Not accepting your polarities therefore means that one side of you is left dormant and cannot be activated to bring about a sense of balance. Below are ways that you can embrace the other half of you, and feel a deeper sense of wholeness.

If you have more masculine energy, connect to your anima by doing the following:

- Listen with the intention of understanding where the other person is coming from.
- Find a hobby, sport, or interest that you are passionate about.
- Tap into your sensual side by practicing romantic gestures.
- Nurture something, like a pet, plant, or child.
- Find creative ways to express yourself, such as drawing, learning a musical instrument, practicing a dance routine, or preparing a new recipe.
- Journal about your thoughts and feelings, or find a trusted therapist who you can talk to.
- Practice self-care by spending time alone, getting sufficient sleep, living an active lifestyle, and setting healthy boundaries.

If you have more feminine energy, connect to your animus by doing the following:

- Practice communicating assertively.
- Find someone to mentor (or find a leadership role in your community).
- Set meaningful goals and hold yourself accountable to achieve them.
- Practice being more self-sufficient (e.g. paying bills on time, improving time management skills, taking care of your household

responsibilities).
- Learn a new practical life skill.
- Practice critical thinking, like weighing the pros and cons of a situation or making decisions based on factual evidence.

Stage 4: Wise Man

When you are free to express every aspect of who you are, there is a special kind of empowerment you feel. The inner void or disconnect is gone, and suddenly you are able to express all types of thoughts and emotions without any resistance. There are no hang-ups in displaying anger, joy, or sadness—or even recalling memories that trigger these emotions. You begin to appreciate the uniqueness of your life story and find meaning in your personal suffering.

According to Jung, the archetype activated during this stage is the wise man. When you think of a wise man, think of someone who has gained life experience and has a grounded approach to life. They embrace different views and opinions because they are not afraid of being wrong, or learning something new about themselves.

To assess how much you have discovered about yourself thus far, below are wise self-reflection questions to explore:

- What have you done, and continue to do in your life, that works for you? What are the signs that it is working?

- What negative habits are you aware of that you need to let go? What obstacles are preventing you from letting them go?

- Think of a childhood struggle that you have survived. What lesson or lessons have you learned from that struggle?

- Which relationships in your life feel safe and loving? What has it taken to create safety in these relationships?

- Which relationships in your life need more forgiveness? What would it take for you to practice forgiveness in each of these relationships?

Stage 5: Self-Consciousness

Self-consciousness is the pinnacle of wholeness. When you are self-conscious, you are aware of who you are and why you react to life the way you do. This doesn't mean that you are flawless, but instead that you are aware of your strengths and flaws. At this stage, you are able to practice self-compassion and accept both good and bad accepts of who you are. This in turn makes it possible to empathize with others and be less judgmental of their flaws and bad traits.

It takes going through these five stages to complete the process of individuation. As you can tell, this journey isn't one that can be completed overnight. It will take time to address past social conditioning, make sense of and acknowledge childhood traumas, heal emotional wounds, and eventually see yourself as an integrated being. Nonetheless, each step of this journey offers healing and helps you become a better version of yourself.

4

End the Terror of Obsessive Thinking

"Yes, I am a prisoner of sorts, but my prison isn't the house. It's my own thoughts that lock me up!"

— V.C. ANDREWS

What Does Obsession Have to Do With Codependency?

In the previous chapter, we looked at real-life examples of codependency in different kinds of relationships. While each type of relationship had its own unique dynamic (E.g. parent-child versus employee-employer), there was a common thread running through all of them—the obsession with the other person.

Codependency issues make it tough for the giver to be themselves. After all, who are they apart from their loved one? Instead of openly expressing who they are, they try to predict what the taker might want to hear or feel, and adopt those thoughts and feelings. Since their self-image is largely based on their role of serving the taker, the giver spends a lot of time thinking about what the taker needs.

It is natural to think about someone you care about a few times a day. When you eat lunch, you might wonder if they have eaten. Or when the weather changes, you hope they packed a jacket in their work bag. Codependent people spend a disproportionate amount of time thinking about their loved ones, to the extent of getting distracted from their own work or life commitments.

The giver in the relationship might structure their lives around the taker. The decisions made about their personal life depend on what is good for the other person in the relationship. For example, a giver may turn down a promotion at work, if it means there will be traveling involved, and they will be forced to spend days away from their loved one. Or they may throw away a certain type of clothing (e.g. short dresses) that make their loved one feel uncomfortable, regardless of how they feel wearing the clothing.

The obsession to make the taker happy and comfortable stems from early childhood conditioning, where the giver received the following subconscious messages from their primary caregiver:

- "Your needs don't matter."
- "I am the number one priority in your life."
- "You are selfish for thinking about yourself."
- "You are responsible for taking care of the family."
- "Taking care of me is normal."
- "Expressing your feelings is not safe."

The subconscious messages written above explain the obsession that givers develop with takers. Since childhood, the giver was conditioned to believe that self-sacrifice was the only way to nurture important relationships in their life. Spending time thinking about their own needs brought about anxiety about the well-being of the other person. Would the parent be able to cope without their obsessive caretaking? Or would they react with anger and withhold love?

Characteristics of Obsessive Personalities

It is important to emphasize that codependent people don't choose to constantly worry about their loved ones. They are terrorized by involuntary and obsessive thoughts about their loved one's safety and happiness.

If they had a choice in the matter, they would invest most of that time and energy into building themselves up and responding to their own needs. But since prioritizing others was ingrained in them from a young age, they cannot help but possess obsessive traits.

An obsessive personality, medically referred to as "purely obsessional OCD" is a mental health condition recognized in the DSM-5. It is a variant of obsessive-compulsive disorder (OCD), and is characterized by "repeated, intrusive, and uncontrollable thoughts that usually have no outwardly related behavioral compulsions" (Christiansen, 2020).

Instead of displaying outward rituals, they develop mental rituals that involve reviewing information, over and over again. For instance, they might review past childhood memories, or recent interactions with others, and create stories about how that life event or interaction could have turned out differently. The stories could be centered around standing up to their abusive parents, expressing their love for a romantic partner, or planning their revenge on people who have hurt them.

Since codependency isn't yet recognized as a mental health condition by the DSM-5, doctors diagnose the patient with co-occurring conditions, like purely obsessional OCD. However, not every individual who suffers from codependency issues will develop this condition. Some may simply adopt obsessive habits or characteristics that cause them to worry about their loved ones constantly.

A few common obsessive traits found in codependent people include:

1. Exaggerated sense of responsibility

A giver believes that without their help and support, the taker won't survive. They have an urge to be the first one to respond to emergencies by sharing advice, taking on others' burdens, and trying their best to fix things. In a controlling way, they may even believe they are the most reliable or knowledgeable person to solve the taker's problems. Taking on so much responsibility can be draining. Even when they feel compelled to help, the giver is left feeling taken for granted.

2. Seeking others' approval

People-pleasing is an obsessive trait because it directs focus outwardly, by seeking to live up to the standards of others. Codependent adults grew up in households where one parent's needs took priority. As kids, they worked tirelessly to please their parent, especially when doing so would earn them affection. They become accustomed to putting other people's needs first and feeling a sense of pride or heightened self-esteem whenever they secure approval.

3. Poor boundaries

Obsessively worrying about another person is a sign of poor boundaries. Codependent people tend to become overly involved in their loved ones' lives, to the extent of being controlling. They struggle with issues of personal space, privacy, or being told "no." Whenever boundary lines are drawn, such as making a request to limit the number of calls per day, they may perceive the limit as a sign of rejection from their loved one.

4. Obsessing over societal roles

Codependent people need to show up correctly to the world, to avoid being criticized or abandoned by others. Consequently, they obsess over their societal roles, such as being a mother, husband, best friend, or boss. Getting these roles right is important for them because it provides a pre-built identity they can hide behind, and use to feel responsible and good about themselves. When they fail at these roles, like breaking up with a friend, they can experience a lot of anxiety. Questions like, "Who am I without this identity?" or "Am I good enough?" expose their core fear of rejection.

5. Transactional approach to relationships

Relationships are a tool that codependent people use to find a sense of purpose and meaning. Saying that relationships mean everything to them, is an understatement. Not only do they throw themselves at every relationship (even new ones), they have high expectations for them to provide a sense of validation or meaning. In exchange for providing a sense of validation or meaning, the codependent person will provide extreme caretaking. They will hold onto those relationships, regardless of how unhealthy they are, for as long as they derive some sort of validation or value from being with the other person.

These obsessive traits are not a life sentence. You are able to recover from them, recognizing and seeking support. Later on in the chapter, we will revisit the four stages of codependency recovery, and look at how you can follow them to heal from obsessive tendencies.

Obsessive Love Disorder

Obsessive love disorder (OLD) is a condition that causes sufferers to become obsessed with a person whom they are in love with. Their primary focus is directed to their loved one, and will often go to great lengths to protect them.

Codependency doesn't cause OLD, however, it can make you vulnerable to it. Some of the early signs of the condition to look out for include:

- Being overly attracted to one person.
- Going from "complete stranger" to "romantic partner" extremely quickly.
- Constantly thinking about the other person throughout the day.
- Feeling the need to protect your loved one, even from their own friends and family.
- Seeing your loved one as your possession, someone who belongs to you.
- Feeling intense jealousy when your loved one interacts with other males and females.
- Constantly having doubts about your loved one's faithfulness or trustworthiness.

Similar to codependency, someone who suffers from OLD may struggle to take rejection. To avoid their loved one leaving, they create relationship rituals. For instance, the OLD person may call or text repeatedly during the day and get upset when their partner cannot be reached. Or they might expect their partner to share their location and whereabouts whenever they are not with them. These rituals are disguised as ways to develop closeness and intimacy. However, in reality, they are tactics used to monitor and control the other person.

The Difference Between Love and Obsession

In popular culture, the idea of someone being obsessed with a loved one sounds, well, romantic. The famous "ride or die" archetypal couple defines what many romantic relationships are like in this modern age. Two individuals enter a relationship (in most cases a codependent relationship) willing to sacrifice everything to prove their love.

The test of love, many believe, is seen in how much difficulty you are able to withstand in a relationship. There is an expectation to accept someone's flaws, and help them heal from their past trauma or present day challenges. While nobody enters a relationship being perfect, the modern understanding of love promotes codependency, and opens the door to obsession and abuse.

Due to movies, reality TV shows, and social media influencers, who glamorize codependent relationships, many of us have forgotten the difference between being in love, versus being obsessed with someone. So, what is love?

Love is a strong emotion that causes you to attach to someone else. You feel a powerful attraction or affection toward someone, and desire to take care of them. A loving relationship creates a physically and emotionally safe environment for two unique individuals to bond and feel accepted by each other. Neither of them try to dominate each other, or assume authority in the relationship.

Obsession, on the other hand, is the need to possess or control something or someone. Many times, obsession doesn't start out as a dark emotion. During the early stages of a relationship, the obsessed partner may display extreme passion. They feel enamored by the other person, and may even put them on a pedestal. Being with the person fulfills a core need, such as feeling worthy, validated, or powerful.

However, as the relationship progresses, the passion turns into possessiveness. The obsessed partner doesn't believe they can survive without the other person in their life, and will do whatever they can to make sure their partner remains dependent on them. Obsessive relationships also tend to have a power imbalance, which by the way is intentional.

In order to make it harder for the other person to leave, the obsessed person will seek dominance by controlling resources, limiting access to friends and family, or making all the decisions. Whenever their sense of control is threatened, they may experience extreme jealousy, paranoia, or become abusive.

Loving relationships shouldn't breed insecurities. They should feel like a refuge, where you can let your guard down and freely express who you are. The couple should seek ways of providing positive reassurance to one another, but never feel responsible for playing the role of fixer or rescuer. Both the act of giving and receiving love should be a choice. For instance, you should be able to choose to enter a committed relationship, respond to your partner's needs, and share aspects of your life with them.

Obsessive relationships don't provide couples with a choice to give and receive love. The obsessed person places expectations on their partner to fulfill certain needs. This creates a toxic situation, where the relationship revolves around one person—the one with greater control. It quickly stops becoming about two individuals feeling safe and accepted, and instead becomes about one individual seeking control and the other one feeling trapped and suffocated.

How to Treat Obsessive Love Disorder

OLD can be treated through taking a variety of interventions. The first step is to seek a medical diagnosis from a doctor. Since there isn't specific medication to treat OLD, you may be prescribed antianxiety medication (e.g. Xanax or Valium), antidepressants (e.g. Prozac, Zoloft, or Paxil), mood stabilizers, or antipsychotics.

You may benefit from taking psychotherapy, to identify and address obsessive thoughts, feelings, and behaviors, as well as understand the impact of your early childhood attachment on your current adult relationships. A qualified therapist will teach you positive coping skills to reduce obsessive thoughts, practice mind-body relaxation, and find healthy distractions.

You can also manage obsessive thinking by going through the four stages of codependency, which are outlined below.

Confronting Obsessive Thinking With the Four Stages of Codependency Recovery

In Chapter 1, we looked at the four stages of codependency recovery: abstinence, awareness, acceptance, and action. While these four stages are generally used to treat codependency as a whole, they can also address specific codependent behaviors that you seek to resolve, such as obsessive thinking.

Below is an example of how you can practice the four stages to reduce obsessive thinking:

Stage 1: Abstinence

Abstinence is about restraining from doing something that is habitual or enjoyable. In the case of obsessive thinking, you would make an effort to restrain from thinking about the other person altogether.

This may be difficult, especially because you have developed a habit of excessive thinking or worrying about them. However, just as you learned the habit by repeating specific behaviors, you can unlearn it by practicing different behaviors.

A great dialectical behavioral therapy (DBT) technique that you can practice to abstain from obsessive thinking is called "opposite action." The aim is to do the exact opposite behaviors of what your thoughts and feelings encourage you to do. For instance, if you feel the urge to text, switch off your phone for 30 minutes. Or when an urge to worry about the person comes up, distract yourself by doing a household chore.

Opposite action isn't a way of pushing down your thoughts and feelings. After all, you need to be aware of the obsessive thought in order to choose an opposite action. Instead of pushing down your thoughts and feelings, this technique creates enough distance between you and the stimulus, so that it is easier to deny your urges. It can also relieve stress and anxiety by encouraging you to get out of your head and do something completely different, as a positive distraction.

To practice taking the opposite action, write down a list of your common obsessive thoughts. For each thought, think about the most appropriate opposite action. This could be a positive behavior that you can practice whenever the obsessive thought comes up. Below are a few examples to assist you:

- Whenever you think "I need to take care of them," practice a self-care activity, like going for a haircut, meditating, or cleaning your living space.
- Whenever you think "I'm afraid they are going to leave me," reach out to a close friend or family member for a catch-up call or coffee date.
- Whenever you think "What will our future be like?" find a small goal-related task that you can perform to redirect focus on your future endeavors.

Now it's your turn. Use the examples above to come up with your own suggestions of opposite actions to take whenever you have obsessive thoughts.

Stage 2: Awareness

Awareness is about reflecting on the dynamic of your codependent relationship, and being willing to assess the pros and cons. By nature, codependent relationships are not healthy, but that doesn't mean there aren't any positive elements to it.

Human beings are wired to run toward pleasure and away from pain. This means that even the most toxic relationships offer some type of pleasure, otherwise there would be no incentive for maintaining them. It is important to be honest with yourself about why you obsessively think about your partner, and the fears or incentives that might be fueling your behavior.

Write down what kinds of fears and pleasures you get from worrying about them, putting their needs first, or doing everything possible to prevent them from leaving you. Do your best to examine your behaviors objectively, as though you were an outsider observing someone else's actions. As you seek to understand the intentions and possible benefits of your obsessive thinking, avoid judging or attempting to correct yourself.

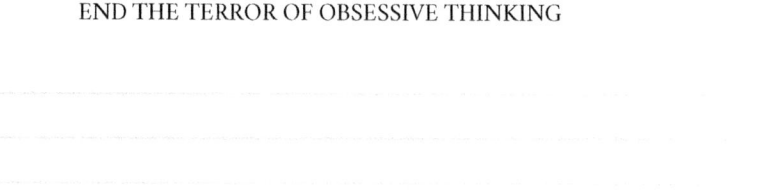

Stage 3: Acceptance

Acceptance is perhaps the most difficult stage of codependency recovery because it involves being okay with who you are. For many givers, who were raised or learned from past experiences to put others' first, self-acceptance can trigger feelings of guilt and shame.

For instance, you might not believe you are deserving of love, hence, your need to obsessively think and worry about others. Or, alternatively, you might think that the only way to receive love is to seek validation from those you sacrificially serve. The beliefs and feelings you may have around self-acceptance can be tough to process and make peace with it.

To help you begin the long process of accepting who you are, here are a few journal prompts that you can work on:

- Where are you saying "yes," when you actually mean to say "no?" What makes saying "no" difficult?

- What is something that you are not allowing yourself to feel?

- What do you need that you are afraid to ask for?

- What can you forgive yourself for?

- What challenging conversation do you need to have with yourself?

- How can you stand up for yourself?

- Which aspects of your personality do you need to make peace with?

- Place your hand on your heart. What does your heart need?

- What can you let go of to significantly improve how you view yourself?

- Where do you need more support?

Stage 4: Action

Taking action is about displaying the proof of what you have learned, and the new beliefs, behaviors, and boundaries you are willing to establish in your life. Remember, taking action is never about proving something to anyone, particularly your codependent partner. It is not a way to gain more attention or change their behaviors.

You are positively changing your obsessive tendencies to improve your quality of life.

Fortunately, reducing obsessive thinking can be done by simply abstaining and finding other positive distractions. However, you may feel that taking some time away from the other person can help you think of them less. You have the right to ask for distance if you believe that will help you address obsessive tendencies. Asking for what you need is part of holding yourself accountable to your commitment.

Be strong and resolute when explaining why you need time away, and trust that you know what's best for you!

There are also a few tips you can practice to keep yourself accountable:

- **Get an accountability partner.** This is a person whose job is to follow up with you and make sure you are staying on track with the commitment you have made. An accountability partner can be a trusted friend or relative, or an unbiased third party, like a licensed therapist.
- **Make self-care a priority.** Activities that promote taking care of your needs can keep you from falling back into old habits of self-harm. Make taking care of yourself a daily practice

through meaningful tasks like getting proper sleep, exercising, or surrounding yourself with positive influences.
- **Call yourself out when you are making excuses.** Be honest with yourself when you are covering up for bad decisions. In a loving way, seek to understand what's stopping you from sticking to your goal. Is it possible that you are afraid of the other person? Or don't have strong belief in yourself? Confront your denial with compassion and seek to resolve whatever is creating a barrier.
- **Create both short and long-term goals.** It is important to be goal-oriented when seeking to replace obsessive thoughts and behaviors. Divide your goals into short and long-term. Your short-term goals can focus on managing your obsessive thinking (i.e. stages one and two of codependency recovery). Then your long-term goals can focus on turning new behaviors into habits, and addressing underlying psychological issues (i.e. stages three and four of codependency recovery). If you believe your life is in danger, your primary focus should be on getting out of the toxic relationship and finding a safe place.
- **Reward yourself.** Be the first person to recognize and celebrate your positive behavioral improvements. You don't need to throw a party; however, take the time to reflect on how far you have come, and how challenging (and meaningful) the journey has been for you. Reward yourself by continuing to prioritize your needs and living your life according to your terms!

Please note that obsessive thinking isn't something you can cure overnight. Like any kind of obsession or addiction, it takes a great deal of time and consistent positive reinforcement to learn healthier behaviors. Continue to practice the four stages of codependency recovery to slowly start changing the way you think and behave.

5

Put Yourself First and Set Boundaries

"Daring to set boundaries is about having the courage to love ourselves even when we risk disappointing others."

— BRENE BROWN

Early Childhood and Boundaries

Boundaries are the invisible lines that separate who you are and what you need, from who others are and what they need. They ensure your values, beliefs, and standards are protected from being violated or disrespected by others.

When you establish proper boundaries to govern different areas of your life, you are able to express who you are with others, without feeling threatened or violated. But in order to establish boundaries, you must first distinguish the difference between healthy and unhealthy behaviors.

This skill may not have been something you were taught as a child, especially if you were raised in a dysfunctional home. As a result, in your adult life, you may be confused about what you should and shouldn't tolerate, or how to speak against harmful behaviors done to you.

No child is born knowing anything about boundaries. The responsibility to teach children how to assert their needs is usually given to parents. Of course, young children will attempt to create their own boundaries by shaking their heads, pushing adults away, or crying. But eventually, as they get older, they will test their parents to see where the boundary lines are, and how much they can get away with.

For children to establish healthy boundaries and feel confident expressing their needs, they must be taught acceptable and unacceptable behavior. Parents create a precedent of what is the "norm" in the household by reenacting certain behaviors in front of their children, showing them what is allowed and forbidden.

In dysfunctional families, good behaviors are not recognized and rewarded enough, while bad behaviors are tolerated and never corrected. This can be confusing to children, who unconsciously learn that there aren't incentives for being good, or ways to hold others accountable for being bad.

Parents in dysfunctional families may also contribute to this confusion by being inconsistent in the types of behaviors they allow and forbid. In most cases, there could even double standards for what is acceptable for parents, but unacceptable for children.

For example, in alcoholic families, where the alcoholic mom or dad is the center of attention, it might be acceptable for them to throw tantrums, but considered unacceptable for their children to display the same emotional outbursts.

Or in families where parents are living with a mental illness, it might be acceptable for them to demand caretaking, but seen as unacceptable for their children to demand the same kind of support and nurturing.

The inability for children to learn and be clear on what is helpful and harmful behavior is what leads to codependency in adulthood—and makes it difficult to establish healthy boundaries. The same way codependent adults tiptoed around their parents and feared confrontation, in the same way they tiptoe around their peers and avoid asserting their needs.

The Need to Address Boundary Violations

Boundary violations are common occurrences for people with codependency issues. You might constantly feel like other people are taking advantage of your kindness, or being inconsiderate of your needs. However, since you are accustomed to placing other people's needs above your own, it is hard to share your true feelings with others, more so when your feelings are negative.

The inability or fear of establishing boundaries may cause you to tolerate any kind of treatment from others. When your feelings have been hurt, you might internalize the anger and frustration, and try not to make a big deal out of it. Most of the time, the people around you may not be aware of how their actions negatively impact you because on the surface, you don't show any signs of being upset or offended.

What is important to remember is that having needs and expressing them to others is natural and normal. Moreover, when people fail to meet your needs, you have the right to acknowledge that you are not receiving something that is important to you, such as respect, support, privacy, or affection. Knowing that you can count on people to respond to your needs is what makes relationships feel safe. Without that knowledge, you may struggle to fully warm up to people.

This also leads us to boundary violations. When a boundary has been violated, you might feel angry, exposed, betrayed, or disrespected. These powerful emotions signal that the relationship doesn't feel safe. In order to restore a sense of emotional safety, it is good to acknowledge what happened and how it made you feel. Express to the other person what boundary they crossed, and what they can do to prevent the same violation in the future.

This conversation is not easy, and in the next chapter, we will look at ways of navigating difficult conversation. However, for now, practice standing up for boundaries and explaining what you need from others. Look into the mirror and show a disapproving expression, or boldly say the words, "I don't like that!" The confidence will come naturally over time, but what matters most is seeing yourself draw the line.

Examples of Boundary Violations and How to Repair Them

Both strangers and loved ones will cross your boundaries. And most times, it may not be intentional. Your job is to learn how to recognize when your boundaries have been crossed, and find ways of regaining a sense of physical and emotional safety.

In this section, we will explore three types of boundaries: physical, emotional, and intellectual. For each, we will discuss what boundary violations look like and how you can address them.

Physical Boundary Violations

Your physical boundaries determine how physically close you desire to be with others. There may be forms of touch that you reserve for specific people only, and feel uncomfortable when others touch you in that manner. For example, kisses may be reserved for your spouse, hugs may be reserved for close friends and family, and with anyone else you prefer handshakes or social distancing.

Examples of physical boundary violations are being physically attacked, deprived of physical touch (i.e. when you are not given the affection you need), as well as when you are touched inappropriately by someone you haven't given consent to. Your body will send signals when physical boundaries have been crossed. For instance, you might freeze, hold your breath, get knots in your stomach, or feel the sensation of your skin crawling.

How to repair boundaries: Ignoring these signals can lead to distrusting your own senses, or perception of danger. After a while of not responding to these violations, you may not show any reaction whenever you are attacked, inappropriately touched, or not given the intimacy you deserve.

Paying attention to your body cues will help you identify when your personal space or body has been invaded, and take action to rebuild your sense of safety. Whenever you are around different people, practice noticing how you feel. How does your body react to being held? How do you feel standing close to them? If you are intimately bonding, what forms of touch make you feel good, and which ones make you feel uncomfortable?

Note that physical boundaries are set depending on how safe you feel around someone, and not the role they play in your life. For example, it is possible to feel unsafe around your siblings, even though you grew up in the same household. Don't be afraid to express discomfort when you are touched inappropriately by a close friend, family member, or coworker. Setting physical boundaries with them doesn't diminish the role they play in your life.

Emotional Boundary Violations

Emotional boundaries separate your needs from other people's needs. Think of them as the protective shield that prevents you from taking on other people's problems or emotions, and adopting them as your own.

The ability to establish strong emotional boundaries is rooted in childhood, particularly in the parent-child relationship. If you were given the space to share your thoughts and feelings, or have different opinions to your parents, then you may be able to take ownership of your emotions, while holding others accountable to theirs.

However, if you were not given the space to share personal thoughts and feelings, but instead were conditioned to think and feel like your parents, it may be difficult for you to determine how you feel about a situation. Whenever someone upsets you, you might feel confused about how to feel or react to the situation. Yes, you may feel angry, but struggle to express yourself, or take ownership of your emotions.

Another example of a poor emotional boundary is allowing others to project their emotions on you. For example, if your friend is upset for personal reasons, you allow them to take out their frustrations on you, through unnecessary arguments, unfair criticism, or other aggressive behaviors. Once again, the inability to draw an emotional boundary is rooted in childhood.

Perhaps you had a parent who was an alcoholic, suffered from bipolar, or had poor emotional regulation skills, and would take out their frustrations on you. Whenever they were upset, the mood in the house would change, and you would feel their wrath. If they were abusive, they may have even said hurtful remarks, like blaming you for their distress or misfortune.

In adult relationships, you might feel personally responsible to keep the other person happy. When they aren't happy, you may feel like you are not doing a good job being there for them. As a way to console the other person, you allow them to dump their emotions on you. The release feels good to them, but unfortunately leaves you feeling drained and responsible for issues that aren't yours to solve.

How to repair boundaries: When your emotional boundaries are violated, relating to others starts to feel unsafe. To protect yourself, you build high walls and defenses, rather than healthy boundaries. Connecting and creating meaningful relationships with people becomes a risk—even with good-intentioned people who desire to show you unconditional love and acceptance.

Emotional boundaries can be repaired by acknowledging your own feelings. If you were raised by parents who often belittled, criticized, or shamed you, being vulnerable and sharing your emotions may not have felt safe. This repeated experience could have taught you to hide, deny, or neglect your emotions, so that you wouldn't feel hurt again.

Acknowledging your feelings is about reopening that aspect of you that once existed as a child. It is about being re-acquainted with the full range of your emotions, and accepting them as valid forms of expressions. Journaling can be a great tool to help you put feelings on paper, and become reacquainted with your emotions. It can even expose recurring emotions and situations that trigger them.

Another aspect of acknowledging your feelings is learning how to affirm your emotional needs. Every human being has emotional needs, which must be maintained in order for relationships to feel safe. Examples of emotional needs include:

- acceptance
- affection
- safety
- trust
- belonging
- empathy
- validation

- kindness
- autonomy
- respect

If the needs above scare you, think about why that is. Could you be deprived of specific needs, and therefore feel apprehensive about asking for them? The relationship with your emotional needs is another theme that you can journal about. You may find that some needs were neglected during childhood, and consequently make you feel uncomfortable.

Nonetheless, not being familiar with your emotional needs, doesn't make them any less important. If you want a challenge, practice looking into a mirror and saying "I need…" followed by one of the needs above. Afterward, mention a sentence about why you need it. For example, "I need respect because I am a unique individual and desire to feel accepted for who I am."

Intellectual Boundary Violations

Intellectual boundaries protect your unique worldviews. They help you understand what you need, value, or believe regarding your life. Healthy intellectual boundaries are flexible enough to allow for learning new information, but assertive enough to interpret the new information based on your ideas and beliefs.

Being raised in a home where your thoughts and opinions are seen as valid, helps you build strong intellectual boundaries as an adult. However, when your outlook on life is too tightly controlled by those around you, you can become dependent on other people's opinions and worldviews.

A typical example is a child who is raised by a codependent parent and lives most of their childhood not making decisions about their life. Every aspect of their day, from when they are going to wake up to what they are going to eat, is decided by their parent. In adulthood, the child may struggle to make life decisions for themselves, and may rely on their parent's or romantic partner's help for most choices that adults would make alone.

Another aspect of an intellectual boundary violation is being told that what you think is wrong or unacceptable. In other words, having someone question your understanding of reality. Not only is this an invasion of your mental space, it can also become a form of manipulation. Gaslighting, for example, is a type of psychological manipulation where the abuser attempts to make you doubt or feel confused about your thoughts and feelings. This is done so that they can distort how you view reality and gain control over your mind.

You have the right to decide on what to think, and how you interpret the world. Be careful of people who make you feel as though your outlook on life is inferior, unrealistic, or something to be ashamed about. Your ideas and beliefs deserve to be treated with respect, and not judged or ridiculed.

How to repair boundaries: Damaged intellectual boundaries cause you to follow whoever is in charge, and adopt their thoughts and beliefs. This puts you in a vulnerable position where you mistrust your own beliefs and struggle to say no to others. Journaling can be a great tool to help you regain confidence in your own ideas. You can reflect on past events and write down your take on what happened and how you felt about it. The privacy and intimacy of journaling can also be a safe way to rebuild trust in your own thoughts.

Another way to repair damaged intellectual boundaries is to remind yourself when listening to others that you can choose to accept or discard what they say. Just because someone speaks with authority, uses a strong tone of voice, or inserts a lot of big words, doesn't mean you have to agree with their view of reality.

Remember, boundaries separate who you are from who others are. It is perfectly okay for others to express their opinions, but unacceptable for them to impose their opinions on you. Practice listening carefully to others and thinking about how much of what they are saying you agree with. If possible, offer your own opinions about the same matter, while creating enough room in the conversation for the others to assert their opinions.

We have looked at three types of boundary violations and how to repair them. The important message to take away from this section is that you are allowed to have needs and wants, no matter how different they may look from the next person's needs and wants. Being comfortable having needs and wants will improve the relationship you have with yourself, which in turn will positively influence the relationships with others.

Why You Should Put Yourself First

Boundaries are a form of self-care that you practice to ensure that your needs are considered in various relationships. They teach you how to show up as your most authentic self and prioritize your well-being.

You may have been taught that putting yourself first is a sign of self-centeredness. However, this is not the case. Selfish people tend to be completely self-absorbed, meaning they fail to regard the needs of others. They see themselves as being the only one, rather than being one of many.

Putting yourself first is a form of caretaking to protect your physical, mental, and emotional health. You show concern about your needs, just as much as you care about the needs of others. In other words, you choose not to neglect yourself at the expense of being present and supportive for other people.

It is understandable why you would feel awkward about the idea of putting yourself first. Perhaps throughout your life, you have been told to put other people's needs first. The result is a disconnect from your deepest needs and desires, which causes you to undermine yourself.

There are a few habits that you can practice to learn how to put yourself first, without feeling overwhelmed by the new attention you are giving yourself. These habits include:

1. Recognize you are worthy

In this superficial world, where everyone is constantly competing and comparing themselves to each other, it can be easy to forget your own self-worth. Make it a habit to remind yourself that you don't need to compromise your needs, desires, or beliefs to be accepted or respected by people. Use positive affirmations to sow uplifting thoughts in your mind. For instance, before going to sleep, close your eyes and repeat the following affirmations:

- I am proud of myself.
- I feel safe in this body.
- My life is getting better.
- I am full of love.

- I accept myself for who I am.

The important thing is to actually believe these affirmations to be true. If there is a part of you that doubts them to be true, journal about where that self-doubt is coming from, and why you find it difficult to see yourself in a positive light.

2. Have regular check-ins

Throughout the day, take two minutes to pause and check-in with yourself. You can do this in between tasks or when you feel a shift in your mood. Simply ask the question: *How are you doing?* And wait for your body to give an answer.

For instance, you might notice dryness in your throat, which signals thirst. Or stomach cramps, which could either be a sign of hunger or digestive issues. On an emotional level, you might notice feeling stressed (an equivalent physical sensation would be a migraine or heart palpitations), or sensing the urge to do something, like take a few deep breaths.

Each time you check in with yourself, there could be different physical and emotional sensations you notice. Some sensations may feel new and unrecognizable. Do a quick Google search of what you are noticing and see what comes up. The information offered could shed some light on what you are experiencing. If you don't have time to respond to your needs immediately, make a note of them and do your best to respond before the day is over.

3. Create a healthy routine

Responding to your physical, mental, and emotional needs is a time-consuming task. To keep up with your daily needs, establish a routine that is tailored according to your priority tasks. Examples of priority tasks would include:

- eight hours of sleep
- three healthy meals a day
- fifteen minutes of cardio exercise
- going to work
- spending time with your pets

Make a commitment, each day, to complete these tasks. Put them first on your list of to-do's, before responding to other people's needs. Avoid making plans during times when you are supposed to be performing your priority tasks. Politely decline the request or invitation, and suggest a more convenient time for you.

Exercise: Self-Care Checklist

Do you know you have a responsibility to take care of yourself? It isn't a luxury, or something that you do whenever you feel like it. The three principles of self-care state that:

1. Failing to respond to your own needs lowers your ability to trust yourself.
2. You are the only person responsible for taking care of yourself, and no situation can justify neglecting your needs.
3. The duty to help others cannot be performed without the duty of self-care.

The best way to improve your level of self-care is to make a checklist of all the needs that are currently being unmet, and for each of them, write down one or two activities you can perform to fulfill those needs.

When deciding on which activities to practice, consider what would be realistic for you, in terms of money, time, and effort. For example, if physical exercise is one of your needs, ask yourself if you are financially able to take out a gym membership, or how much time you can realistically devote to exercise each day. This will help you manage expectations and feel more committed to your practices.

To make your checklist, create a list of unmet needs similar to the one below.

Unmet needs	Activities
Sleep	
Nutrition	
Healthcare	
Physical exercise	
Physical intimacy	
Stress management	
Healthy boundaries	
Personal growth	
Companionship	
Personal time	
Spirituality	

PUT YOURSELF FIRST AND SET BOUNDARIES

For every unmet need, write down an activity that you can perform each day or week to fulfill that need. Remember to make the activities practical and realistic. Below is an example of a completed checklist.

Unmet needs	Activities
Sleep	Go to bed at 09:00 p.m.
Nutrition	Consume a whole foods diet
Healthcare	Schedule a quarterly check-up with your doctor
Physical exercise	Complete a 15-minute cardio workout video
Physical intimacy	Get a professional massage
Stress management	Journal for 15 minutes
Healthy boundaries	Say no whenever you feel like you are overextending yourself
Personal growth	Read a self-help book
Companionship	Join a support group online
Personal time	Take an hour for yourself
Spirituality	Take a 10-minute mindfulness meditation

6

Learn the Art of Assertive Communication

"To be passive is to let others decide for you. To be aggressive is to decide for others. To be assertive is to decide for yourself. And to trust that there is enough, that you are enough."

— EDITH EVA EGER

What It Means to Be a People-Pleaser

A people-pleaser is someone who feels compelled to seek approval from others. They are often not comfortable asserting their own thoughts and feelings, and look to others for reassurance.

Most times, people-pleasing is disguised as showing compassion for others or being considerate of others' needs. However, there is a difference between empathizing with others and being afraid of saying no. People-pleasers don't feel like they have a choice to turn the "nice" switch off. They feel obliged to do favors for others and extend themselves, until the point of exhaustion.

The desire behind people-pleasing is to feel accepted and loved by others. This desire is pure, and often rooted in the lack of acceptance and affection in childhood. To gain friendships and make social interactions a lot smoother, people-pleasers learn to adapt their behaviors to appeal to the people around them. For instance, they can be extraverted around extraverted people, and introverted around introverts. This is how they win people over and form close relationships.

One of the problems brought about by people-pleasing is the inability to share strong thoughts and feelings openly. Communication is filtered to portray a favorable self-image, and conflicting needs or emotions that could lead to disapproval (e.g. anger, stress, resentment, etc.) are hidden. It is therefore difficult to understand how a people-pleaser genuinely feels, what they need, or where their boundary lines are. Even when they are upset, they try very hard not to show it, to avoid any drama or conflict.

Some of the communication issues experienced by people-pleasers include:

- difficulty saying no to others
- taking on extra tasks, even when they are overworked
- overcommitting to social plans and creating excuses for non-attendance
- insist they are fine when they are emotionally distressed
- avoid confrontation or expressing opinions that might not be shared by the group
- agree to go along with plans they are unhappy about to avoid conflict

These communication issues can create a lot of stress for people-pleasers, and consequently lead to the following adverse behaviors:

- pressure to be happy and pleasant all the time
- anxiety about speaking up for themselves
- stress due to overextending themselves to others
- constantly feeling taken for granted
- low self-esteem due to feeling inferior to others

Codependency issues can put you at risk of developing people-pleasing behaviors. However, it is important to note that you can be a people-pleaser without having codependency issues. What makes the two traits similar is the obsessive need to help others, difficulty setting healthy boundaries, and the fear of communicating genuine thoughts and feelings.

If you identify as a people-pleaser, one of the most empowering decisions you can make for yourself is to learn how to communicate effectively with others, and say no when necessary. Like all the other strategies we have discussed so far, being an effective communicator takes skill and practice.

How Codependency Affects Communication

Due to the desire to feel needed, you might struggle to express genuine thoughts and feelings, especially when you believe they might upset the other person. Unlike other people, you have a low tolerance for conflict and cannot stand any kind of disagreement.

The desire to feel needed, coupled with the low tolerance for conflict, often means that you struggle to express anger and frustration, hold others accountable for bad behaviors, or communicate unmet needs. Nonetheless, when you are backed against a corner, you will eventually communicate—but not in a healthy way. Below are four common styles of communication seen in codependent people:

Passive Aggressive Communication

Passive-aggressive communication is a discrete way of expressing aggression without being caught. The aggression is seen through subtle, indirect sabotage or sarcasm. The aim is to appear cooperative, but secretly plot to frustrate someone who has hurt you. Since you feel powerless to confront them head on, you use less obvious ways of showing disapproval.

Resentful Communication

Harboring so much pain from unmet needs, betrayal, and disappointment from others leads to a build-up of resentment. In your mind, you sense there is an inequality in how others treat you, versus how you treat them. For instance, when resolving interpersonal problems, you might use exaggerations like "I always!" and "you never!"

Another tactic is keeping score of what you do for others. You might say things like, "I'm doing more work than you" or "I'm the only one who makes an effort." It is also common to blame others when you feel resentful. Instead of expressing how their actions make you feel, you might say "If you acted differently, this wouldn't have happened" or "You make me feel angry."

Immature Communication

Immature communication is when something is said in a childish way. Think about how a child would react when they are angry. They would make demands like "Do this for me right now!" or make hurtful, impulsive comments like "I hate you!"

A child is also still grappling with their emotions and is unable to separate how they feel from what is happening in the situation. For example, they will assume that just because they feel angry about the situation, like being told to do their house chores, their parents must have done something wrong. In some cases, this is true, but other times their emotions paint a different picture of what is actually happening.

Miscommunication Due to Unclear Needs

Communication is tough when you are confused about your needs, or when you know what you need but fail to articulate it. In relationships, this might look like indecisiveness, going back and forth on a decision, and not being able to reach some kind of resolution.

Another reason which might contribute to the miscommunication is feeling compelled to go along with other people's choices, then feeling lost when you decide to backtrack and do what feels right for you.

For example, you might agree to go on a date with someone, only because it was their idea, and they seemed really excited about it. However, as you spend more time thinking about the date, you realize that it isn't something you are up for. Backtracking on your decision and pulling out on the plan might cause the other person to feel confused and even offended. This makes it harder to follow your heart and do what's right for you.

Strategies to Communicate Assertively

Assertive communication is a way of expressing your thoughts and feelings, while being considerate of another person's thoughts and feelings. In other words, you confidently stand up for yourself, without becoming controlling or disrespectful. Many people confuse assertive communication with aggressive communication, where someone comes off as being pushy or argumentative. However, that is not what assertive communication is about at all.

The assertive communicator's goal is to create win-win situations. They walk into a conversation being mindful of their position, yet open to learn about the other person's position, and how both of them might find middle ground. They don't seek to make demands or manipulate others into following their lead. What they truly want is to be understood and seek to understand where the other person is coming from too.

There are a number of benefits to becoming an assertive communicator. Some of these benefits include:

- Gaining the confidence to express a range of thoughts and feelings openly.
- Feeling less anxious and unprepared to have difficult conversations with others.
- Improving the respect you have for yourself, which causes others to show deeper respect for you.
- Being able to make decisions on your own without requiring assistance from others.

- Feeling a sense of relief knowing that people around you are aware of your needs and boundaries.

Overall, becoming an assertive communicator improves the quality of your relationships. You have the ability to express your needs, set and reinforce boundaries, as well as resolve conflict in a firm, yet empathetic way. Below are five assertive communication strategies that you can practice, over and over again, to express your needs and wants in a positive and respectful way:

1. Use "I" statements

You cannot control how others treat you, but you can control how you respond to them. Using "I" statements, like "I feel" or "I think" shows ownership of your thoughts and emotions. Yes, the situation could have brought about the feeling of anger, but that feeling came from you. The beauty of assertive communication is being able to hold others accountable for their actions without blaming them for how you feel.

Here are a few ways of using "I" statements:

- I feel ignored when you come into the house and don't greet me.
- I felt uncomfortable with the way you spoke to me earlier.
- I get frustrated when you don't give me an opportunity to speak.
- I need you to make more of an effort to help around the house.

Please note that "I" statements can also be used to show appreciation and recognize positive behaviors. For instance, you might say "I feel happy whenever I spend time with you," or "I appreciate the concern you show for me."

2. Learn to say no

Saying no feels uncomfortable, but it is one of the easiest boundaries to set. If simply saying "no" feels too direct for you, there are other assertive ways of expressing disapproval, while being considerate of the next person's feelings. Below are a few suggestions:

- I'm busy right now. Can I call you later?
- I'm sorry, this doesn't work for me.
- I can't take on any new projects right now.
- I don't feel comfortable with this arrangement.
- My schedule is looking full this week. Can we postpone it for next week?

Finding indirect ways of saying no is fine, however, remember to be as clear as possible. Your statement shouldn't leave any room for the other person to assume you meant "yes" or "maybe."

3. Be open to feedback

Assertive communication is a two-way conversation. You start by stating your needs and wants, then allow the other person to share their opinions or expectations. The conversation continues to go back and forth, until you are able to reach a healthy compromise. It is therefore required to allow an opportunity for feedback, but most importantly, be open to hearing what the other person has to say.

Here are a few ways to express your openness to feedback:

- You have heard my perspective. I would like to hear yours too.
- From what I have shared, is there anything you would like to share?
- Based on what I have said, what are your thoughts?
- Is there anything you would like to add?

Be prepared to receive feedback that is contrary to what you want to hear. Remember to respect the other person's intellectual boundaries (their right to have unique thoughts and beliefs), even if you don't agree with them. You can gain more understanding about where they are coming from by asking open-ended questions like "When you say... What do you mean?"

4. Show empathy

Empathy is the ability to step inside someone else's shoes and imagine what they might be thinking or feeling. During a conversation where you are discussing needs or setting boundaries, being empathetic demonstrates a willingness to learn and understand the other person's perspective, so you can find a middle ground.

Some of the ways to show empathy in a conversation include:

- I understand what you are saying.
- I can only imagine how that feels.
- You are making a lot of sense.
- It sounds like you are having a difficult time.
- I can see that you are frustrated.

Acknowledging someone's experience doesn't diminish your request. It simply shows that you care about how a situation impacts them, rather than only getting your needs met.

5. Be mindful of your emotions

What makes assertive conversations effective is their ability to balance logic and emotion. On the one hand, you are clear about the offense committed or need that hasn't been met, and seek to find a solution or establish a boundary. But on the other hand, you are aware of the emotional impact of having your boundaries violated or not being on good terms with the other person.

To maintain the balance of logic and emotion, keep a watchful eye on your emotions. Do your best to monitor how you are feeling during the conversation, by checking-in with yourself and picking up on body cues. Becoming overly emotional will cloud your judgment and cause the other person to become defensive. The conversation will turn into a blame game, and neither of you will walk away feeling understood.

Whenever you sense that you are getting too emotional, excuse yourself from the conversation and take five minutes to cool down. Take three deep mindful breaths and return when you have regained a sense of control. If you notice the other person becoming increasingly emotional, suggest a break or postpone the conversation to another time. It isn't good for both of you to feel pressured to give a response or continue a conversation that is starting to feel aggressive.

7

Improve Your Relationship With Fear

"I think sometimes making yourself vulnerable before you are ready is exactly what can hold you accountable. Do what you fear."

— BRITTANY BURGUNDER

Is Fear the Real Enemy?

A few years back, I purchased an alarm system for my house. I remember being adamant to buy one that had the latest technology— I'm talking motion sensors and the works!

After installing the device, I didn't get any sleep for a week. Every night, upon activating the alarm, I would be woken up by loud sirens going off. Apparently the device was so sensitive that it could pick up on dust and leaves blowing past. I called the company and had my security settings adjusted so that I could finally get my peaceful night's rest!

Imagine if I decided to throw away my security system altogether because of how frustrated it made me feel. Would that have been the best decision?

Your relationship with fear is much like having an annoying security system installed in your body. Since you have a history of surviving adverse life experiences, your built-in security system is highly sensitive to potential threats. It may keep you up at night, cause you to lose focus at work, or make it hard for you to develop healthy relationships—all because of false alarms constantly going off!

Of course, you have options. Do you throw away the security system altogether and expose yourself to real and imagined threats, or do you attempt to adjust the settings so that you aren't constantly on high alert?

Feeling on edge and stressed all the time can be exhausting! Sometimes, it seems better to just disown your fears altogether. However, there is a biological benefit to feeling afraid. When you feel afraid, you are able to think on your feet, seek professional help, escape dangerous relationships, and identify emotional wounds that haven't been healed.

Disowning your childhood fears won't solve your relationship problems, neither will it make you feel safer bonding with others. The real issue isn't the fact that you are afraid, but that you haven't found ways of addressing your fears and getting the closure you deserve.

Fear isn't the enemy that you have made it out to be.

In fact, once you change your perspective, you will find that your fears once brought you a lot of comfort and security in a time when you didn't have anyone to turn to. However, now that you are ready to heal, you no longer need to hide behind the fear, or fear-based coping mechanisms. You can embrace your fears and accept them as being real experiences, without identifying with them anymore.

Are you ready to experience this kind of freedom?

Healing From Codependency Fears

Codependency and anxiety go together. You have a tendency of worrying about other people's emotional states or problems, without even realizing it. Whenever you sense another person's discomfort, you can feel upset or responsible for restoring their sense of balance. Taking on that excessive amount of distress upon your shoulders can trigger your body's stress response, bringing up personal childhood fears that may not have anything to do with their situation.

A common example that occurs in romantic relationships is feeling a sense of rejection when your partner is in a bad mood that is unrelated to you, or your relationship. Seeing them suffer in that way sends alarm bells ringing in your body. Your immediate thought is, "something is not right, and I am responsible for fixing it."

If you are unable to fix their mood by making them feel better, another thought might arise in your head, "They are feeling upset because of me." This second thought is a sign that a deeper fear—the fear of rejection—has been triggered by your anxious feelings.

You might wonder what is important to address first: your anxious feelings or the underlying fears that are triggered every time you feel anxious? If you are looking for a long-term solution, addressing your underlying fears can make it easier to cope with stress and manage your strong emotional reactions.

Addressing your core fears won't be easy, nor will it feel comfortable all the time. This is because you have spent many years running away from, or seeking to numb, your fears. Now that you are ready to confront them, you can be taken back to past childhood experiences that were painful to go through. However, as you courageously take this step to face your fears, remember that you are an adult now. You are no longer living the life of that younger version of you, and therefore you can reflect on their life experiences without reliving the past.

The following section will present a common childhood fear that is typical of people who are experiencing codependency issues: the fear of rejection. You will learn about the fear in more depth, so you can understand what exactly you are afraid of, then receive strategies on how you can start conquering the fear of rejection.

Conquering the Fear of Rejection

Rejection is a risk that doesn't pay off. What makes this experience painful, is the difficulty accepting things not working out. It takes so much courage to open up, step outside your comfort zone, and show vulnerability. For someone with codependency issues, putting yourself out there like this doesn't happen every day.

When your risk doesn't pay off, you are reminded of all the childhood risks that didn't pay off, like trusting your parents to provide a sense of security, opening your heart to a boy or girl who ended up breaking your heart, or seeking out work opportunities that ended in failure. There are few factors that make you more sensitive than others to things not working out. These factors include:

1. Childhood trauma

Unresolved feelings of experiencing rejection as a child can make you sensitive to rejection as an adult. Examples of adverse events that may have led to feelings of rejection include losing a loved one, living with a single parent (or witnessing a separation), being treated less than other siblings, or being raised by a parent who was unable to show unconditional love.

2. Low self-esteem

If you already feel worthless or inferior to others, then even the slightest amount of disregard, or someone saying no, can make you feel rejected. Moreover, having a low self-esteem can cause you to attract people who are dominant or seek dominance in a relationship. You may repeat much of the same attachment patterns exhibited in the relationship with your parents, and make it your mission to seek approval or affection from them.

3. Negative core beliefs

As a child, you make up stories about what the world is like, based on the kind of "world" created in your household. These stories become ingrained in your mind and become core beliefs. Negative core beliefs are disempowering stories that you have told yourself about the world and others. They might include things like:

- The world is a dangerous place.
- People can't be trusted.
- Love must be earned.
- People always leave.

In adult relationships, these negative core beliefs are triggered whenever you are stressed, feel anxious, or experience failure. Rooting out these negative core beliefs requires you to change the narrative.

It is possible to conquer the fear of rejection. But beware, it will not make you immune from experiencing rejection in the future. Unfortunately, rejection is a part of life. At some point or another, someone will disappoint you, or you may disappoint someone. It is unrealistic to think that every relationship will be healthy, or will satisfy every need.

Nevertheless, you don't have to allow the fear of being rejected to hinder you from building healthy relationships and learning to trust others. One way to conquer the fear of rejection is to address your limiting beliefs.

Overcome Your Limiting Beliefs

Limiting beliefs are negative assumptions about yourself or others that provoke certain fears, such as the fear of rejection. Depending on how strong your limiting belief is, it has the power to prevent you from pursuing career opportunities, building new relationships (or leaving unfulfilling relationships), or living the life you desire.

Limiting beliefs may be centered around how you view yourself and how you view the world. Beliefs about yourself can negatively impact your self-esteem and cause you to feel a sense of shame and rejection, as though there is something inherently wrong with you.

For example, you might think that you are:

- less intelligent than others
- socio-economically disadvantaged
- too old or too young to pursue certain goals
- too ugly to attract companionship
- too psychologically damaged to maintain a healthy relationship

Note that these beliefs don't need to be true for you to feel like they are. For example, you may be doing really well for yourself in life and have a strong support system, yet still have a nagging feeling like people don't like you.

But limiting beliefs about the world can be equally destructive, and cause you to lose hope or trust in humanity. They mostly focus on what you think people will or won't allow you to access, what other people think of you, or questioning what exists and what doesn't exist.

For example, you might think:

- People respond negatively to you because of your different personality.
- You can't access certain opportunities, like going to university or applying for your dream job because of previous life disadvantages.
- Life favors people who demonstrate specific traits that you may not possess.
- True love between two people doesn't exist.
- Human beings are selfish and will always find a way of disappointing you.

Overcoming your limiting beliefs takes introspection. You are the best person to ask the tough questions and challenge beliefs that you once created in your mind to make sense of the world.

Here are three questions that can help you confront and overcome your limiting beliefs:

What If You Are Wrong?

Has it ever crossed your mind that you could be wrong about your limiting beliefs? That they may be based on false assumptions, rather than facts? Limiting beliefs tend to create black-and-white outcomes. For instance, you are either ugly or beautiful, poor or rich, weird or normal. These black-and-white outcomes are not true representations of reality, nor are they fair conclusions to draw about yourself.

Bring up a limiting belief related to your fear of rejection. Ask yourself the question: *What if I'm wrong?* On the lines below, provide evidence for and against your belief. Shift away from black-and-white thinking and try to present the full picture.

_____

_____

_____

_____

How Is This Belief Serving You?

What is the benefit of holding onto a belief that makes you feel afraid to trust yourself or others? You might think that there isn't any, but if that was the case, why would you continue to reinforce it? Beliefs are created to protect your perception of reality. They make life feel safer, or more bearable. Even limiting beliefs serve some kind of purpose.

Think about another limiting belief (not the same as the one above) related to your fear of rejection. Figure out what purpose it is serving in your life. Could there be some benefit of holding onto this belief?

What's the Alternative?

Your beliefs are not set in stone. As you grow and gain new insight about yourself, your beliefs can adapt to reflect your fresh outlook. There is always "another side" to a limiting belief. The other side is often a more fair and balanced perspective. It seeks to evaluate life without leaning too heavily on negative or positive outcomes.

An alternative doesn't need to be complicated. It can be as basic as substituting "can't" with "can" or "never" with "not yet." For example:

- "I can't maintain healthy relationships" turns to "I can maintain healthy relationships."
- "I will never know what true love feels like" turns to "I haven't experienced true love yet."

Tell yourself that you don't need to settle for your limiting beliefs. You have plenty of options on how you decide to experience life. If your belief isn't motivating enough, ask yourself: What's the alternative?

Think about a third limiting belief that you hold (different from the first two) related to your fear of rejection. Write down at least three alternative beliefs to replace it with.

_____

_____

_____

Finally, choose at least one alternative belief to test. Spend a week reflecting on the belief, rehearsing it to yourself, and behaving in ways that support it.

Notice how natural and realistic it feels. If you find that it isn't a good fit or feels superficial, test another alternative belief. Do this until you find an alternative belief that resonates with you and feels as comfortable as a new pair of jeans!

The Power in Accepting Your Fears

In this chapter, we focused on one fear related to codependency. However, there are many others that you may be living with, such as the fear of criticism, failure, vulnerability, not being good enough, or feeling out of control. Overcoming your limiting beliefs can help you address these other fears too; however, another incredibly powerful strategy is to accept your fears for what they are, rather than disowning them.

Have you wondered what would happen if you accepted your fears? Is that even something you can imagine right now?

Coming to a place of acceptance is a journey. There are many pit stops that you make along the way, such as acknowledging and healing childhood traumas, rediscovering who you are separate from your wounded self, and finally embracing your life for the beauty and chaos that it brings.

Eventually, you will reach the point of coming to terms with your fears. This moment can be both exhilarating and terrifying. For the first time you can imagine a healthy life that isn't governed by trauma-informed coping mechanisms, but since you have never lived without fear, the thought of not having things to be watchful for is discomforting.

Nevertheless, what becomes clear to you is the need for healing and breaking old cycles, so you proceed anyway.

Accepting your fears feels like making peace with parts of yourself that you have been fighting against for many years. The war against yourself is finally over, and you can reconcile different aspects of you, and accept them as one united whole.

Unfortunately, there is not much more I can say about the experience of accepting your fears because there is no formula to reach that point, nor does the experience look the same for each individual. However, what I can say is that going through the codependency recovery journey and learning to view your life with greater compassion and non-judgment, can help you come closer to making peace with your fears. Do the inner work. It's worth it!

Exercise: Processing Fears With Inner Child Work

An ongoing exercise that you can practice as you continue the codependency recovery journey and process your fears is inner child work. The inner child is the unhealed aspect of your subconscious mind that is carried from childhood to adulthood. It remembers childhood experiences, both good and bad, and often seeks closure for unresolved emotional wounds.

Since the inner child isn't a real person, it seeks closure by bringing up painful memories or triggering strong emotions that lurk in your subconscious mind. You can imagine this as a real child who throws a tantrum to get the attention of their parents.

Likewise, your inner child is yearning for your attention. It knows that you are the only person who can go back in time and heal past wounds through acknowledging and releasing them. It also knows that you are old enough to re-parent that neglected part of you, and offer yourself the love and nurturing that you were deprived of.

Below are a few exercises to begin the inner child work:

Describe Your Inner Child

Have you met your inner child before? If not, why not start off by getting acquainted with them?

The best way to connect to your inner child is to recall the earliest traumatic event. Your inner child was born after this event. Ever since then, they have been seeking support to heal from various traumatic experiences.

As you reflect the earliest traumatic event, try and answer the following questions about your inner child:

- How old is he/she?
- What is your inner child wearing?
- What expressions does your inner child have on his/her face?
- How is he/she feeling?
- What secrets is he/she keeping?

Describing your inner child will help you create a mental image that you can frequently bring up whenever you are seeking to connect with this part of you.

Affirm Your Inner Child

Your inner child felt most of the strong emotions you felt as a child: neglected, lonely, unworthy, or unloved. Since nobody reaffirmed you back then that you were safe, intelligent, creative, and worthy of affection, you can offer your inner child that kind of validation to silence some of their doubts.

To affirm your inner child, close your eyes and imagine yourself hearing the following statements, spoken in a soft, warm, and loving voice:

- I am happy you are alive.
- I need you.
- I love you.
- You are so special to me.
- I love every quality in you.
- You make me proud.
- Thank you for being you.
- You are safe with me.
- I enjoy being around you.
- You are important to me.

Identify which statements caused the strongest emotional reactions within you. Make a note below of those statements and reflect on why those specific statements mean so much to hear.

Explore Your Inner Child's Beliefs

Think of a hurtful childhood experience that involves your parents, and answer the following questions:

- Write down keywords to describe how the experience made you feel. E.g. scared, rejected, betrayed, judged, etc.

- Write down keywords to describe how your parents responded or treated you. E.g. cold, self-centered, moody, aggressive, controlling, etc.

- What words or comments did your parents make? E.g. "You are a burden!"

- What disapproving facial expressions or body language did your parents give? E.g. tight lip, frown, crossed arms, etc.

- What story did you come up with about yourself after the experience? E.g. I am difficult to love.

8

Decide to Stay or Leave

"Courage isn't having the strength to go on – it is going on when you don't have strength."

— NAPOLEON BONAPARTE

Can Codependent Relationships Work?

A common misconception people have about codependent relationships is that there is no love present at all. This idea is wrong. Like any other type of relationship (i.e. romantic, parent-child, work, or social relationship), there is some degree of intimacy that exists. Of course, unlike healthy relationships, this intimacy is often clouded by harmful behaviors that make one or both parties feel unsafe.

Therefore, when discussing the subject of ending codependent relationships, we must be sensitive to the fact that there may be genuine bonds between two individuals that aren't easy to break.

If you are at a crossroads, deciding whether to stay or leave a codependent relationship, understand that it is normal to go back and forth on your decision. Finally pulling the plug and deciding to go no contact with the person is never taken lightly.

Instead of applying pressure on yourself to make a quick decision, spend some time thinking about your options, and reimagining life without your partner, friend, family member, or colleague. It may also help to consider the possibility of your relationship actually working out, and how both you might be able to turn things around.

Here's a question you may have not asked yourself before: *What would it take to heal your codependent relationship?*

Seriously think about this question, and write a list of all the changes that you and the other individual would need to make.

Your list will have several points of behavioral changes that need to take place. Some of the changes will need to come from you and others from them. However, without both of you being able to recognize the need for change, the dynamic of your relationship will stay the same.

What's crucial to understand about unhealthy behaviors is that they don't disappear overnight. They are usually a symptom of harmful thoughts, beliefs, and attitudes that have existed for many years. Unfortunately, being aware of your loved one's problematic behaviors doesn't erase them either. They must go through the four stages of codependency recovery (i.e. abstinence, awareness, acceptance, and action) to begin confronting years' worth of maladaptive coping mechanisms.

Why is this important to note? Because as someone with codependency issues, you might fall into the trap of thinking you can fix or rebuild the other person. This assumption is not true. As heartwarming as your presence may be in their lives, staying in the relationship for the sake of "fixing" them will not correct their behaviors.

Not only do they need to recognize the need for change, they must also be open and motivated to change—and take the necessary steps to enforce the change (i.e. going to counseling). The action (as outlined in stage four of recovery) has to come from them, otherwise we cannot truly say they are motivated to change.

Something else that you may want to think about is whether the other person is mentally and emotionally fit for a healthy relationship. As mentioned throughout the book, it is common to find one or both people in a codependent relationship who are suffering from mental illness or substance abuse problems. What this means is that even if they might recognize the need for change and feel motivated to change, the simple fact that they are not well can make it difficult for them to go through the stages of codependency recovery.

Perhaps before thinking about saving the relationship, both of you can discuss getting on a treatment plan to address mental health issues. The other person's state of mind and quality of life should be one of the first interventions taken, if both of you desire to stay in the relationship.

With all this said, I do believe that codependent relationships can work. But there is a lot of time and healing that must take place in order for the dynamic to change. Both parties must recognize the need for behavioral changes, and be willing to take the necessary actions. Moreover, any current and underlying mental and emotional health issues should be dealt with first to ensure that the new dynamic built feels safe and healthy.

Signs That Your Relationship Is Harmful

While I agree that codependent relationships can sometimes work, there are cases when it is better to walk away. Of course, this decision isn't taken lightly, especially when there is a long history between the individuals. But when the relationship begins to negatively affect your physical, mental, and emotional well-being, there is more to lose by staying than leaving.

Below are a few signs that your relationship has become unhealthy, and possibly life-threatening:

- **Your partner/friend/relative/colleague constantly finds something to criticize you about.** Someone who is always finding fault in you can slowly damage your sense of self-worth. After a while of repeatedly listening to their negative or sarcastic words, you may start to take what they say as being the truth.
- **There is a noticeable imbalance of power.** There is a clear distinction between who has most of the control in the relationship. This creates an unhealthy union where one person feels superior and dominant over the other. The imbalance of power can also justify harmful, oppressive behaviors practiced on the submissive person.
- **Your partner/friend/relative/colleague is excessively jealous.** When their jealousy reaches a point where they seek to monitor your movements, request device passwords, control what you wear, or who you have access to, it is a clear sign of an abuse of power, and that the relationship has become toxic.

- **Your partner/friend/relative/colleague fails to take responsibility for their actions.** The lack of accountability is not a positive sign that any behavioral changes can take place in the near future. When they struggle to apologize and admit their mistakes, it shows a disregard for your needs and hurt feelings. In such an environment, it may be hard for you to feel safe and supported.
- **Your partner/friend/relative/colleague uses manipulation tactics to control you.** Did you know that any type of manipulation is a form of abuse? Even something that many people overlook like giving the silent treatment. Manipulation tactics are used to gain control over another person's actions or emotions. What makes them so dangerous is that over time they can cause mental and emotional damage (e.g. anxiety, depression, eating disorders, substance abuse problems, etc.).

Some of these signs may not be noticeable in your relationship. Or maybe the positive moments you share somehow make the bad times appear less damaging. To truly rule out any possible signs of toxicity in your relationship, spend a month documenting how you feel around the other person.

After spending time with them, record how you felt before, during, and after your encounter. Be honest with your assessments, and just write what you felt in your body. Try not to analyze your notes until the month is up. Thereafter, sit down with a trusted friend or licensed therapist and go over your records.

Five-Step Plan to Leave a Codependent Relationship

So you have decided to exit your codependent relationship? I applaud you for such an enormous display of courage. Even though your mind is made up, the process of leaving your loved one can feel terrifying and confusing. Below are five steps to prepare you to safely get out of a codependent relationship.

Step 1: Look in the Mirror

Before you get up and walk away, look at yourself in the mirror. Recognize the role you played in creating this unhealthy relationship dynamic, and acknowledge the various problems that have motivated your decision to leave. If there have been any wrongdoings that you have committed against the other person, write a forgiveness letter to them (you are not forced to share it with them). And if there were any wrongdoings you committed against yourself, write yourself a personal letter asking for forgiveness.

You are welcome to write your forgiveness letter below.

Step 2: Have the Difficult Conversation

If you feel safe enough to have the conversation face-to-face, then schedule an appropriate time where both of you can meet. If possible, meet at a communal space, like a restaurant, which is neutral and public.

Anticipate the conversation going in a multitude of ways, and have a plan for when tensions start running high. For example, if the other person starts to raise their voice, your plan might be to set a boundary. But if their behavior exceeds that and becomes more aggressive, you can plan on walking away and resuming the conversation via text or email.

Another option that might work for both of you is having a mediator, such as a counselor, present in the room while you are having the conversation. They may be able to assist in diffusing the tension and making sure both of you get equal opportunity to voice your thoughts and feelings.

Do you have a plan B for when the conversation doesn't go as expected? Write it down below.

_____

_____

_____

_____

Step 3: Focus on Self-Care

The weeks and months following the break-up are important days of self-care. Not only is putting yourself first a positive distraction, it is also a good way to start training your mind to accept the new norm. The four stages of codependency recovery will come in handy during this time—so will staying connected to your friends and family and seeking medical support for any physical, mental, or emotional issues.

Create a list of your favorite self-care activities that target your physical, mental, and emotional well-being.

Step 4: Continue to Read About Codependency

Even though the storm is over, and you are probably feeling a lot safer now, it is important to continue studying your codependency issues. If you are attending therapy sessions, this is something that your therapist can assist you with. Alternatively, you can purchase books, courses, or listen to videos that shed light on codependency, and the various ways to recover from it.

Step 5: Develop Your Sense of Self-Worth

The final step is an ongoing step that you will continue to practice (and be mindful of) throughout your life, and in the new relationships you form. Find ways to reinforce a positive sense of self-worth, like practicing self-care, cultivating self-acceptance, reinforcing healthy boundaries, setting aspirational goals, or making a meaningful contribution in the lives of others. There is no such thing as having "too many reasons" to love and value the person that you are!

So, will you feel healed after practicing these five steps? Maybe or maybe not. What is certain though is the fact that you will be in a better off position than you were when you left the codependent relationship. Remember, healing, like codependency recovery, is a journey that takes time and constant positive reinforcement to complete successfully.

Managing Post-Breakup Grief

A common experience that follows a codependent relationship breakup is grieving the loss of the other person. Indeed, the realization that you don't have access to them anymore can feel as though you are mourning the death of a loved one.

In a way, you are mourning a death—the death of an extremely addictive relationship. Similar to any addict who is going through withdrawal symptoms, you might fall physically sick, or feel depressed.

Being gentle and compassionate toward yourself is vital during this time. Breakups, for people with codependency issues, are extremely painful. This process is likely to make you experience a range of emotions and struggle to feel like yourself for some time. Be mindful of the way you speak to yourself, and how you make sense of what is happening.

Some of the harmful thoughts and emotions that you should attempt to avoid during this time include:

1. Blaming yourself for the breakup

Avoid the temptation to look at the negative outcome of the relationship as being your fault. You are not responsible for the other person's actions, state of mind, or decisions. You cannot fix or rescue them from their self-destructive behaviors, nor was it possible for you to "save" the relationships. While it is true that you are not completely innocent, be fair and level-headed when assessing the part you played in the relationship. Accept your mistakes and be generous to forgive yourself.

2. Feeling a sense of shame

Another emotion that you should avoid at all costs is feeling ashamed for staying in the relationship, or tolerating the harmful behaviors, for as long as you did. If you knew better, and maybe received the psychological tools many years earlier, perhaps you would have left the relationship sooner. Nonetheless, there is no purpose in thinking about what you should have done because you cannot change the past. Focus on the progress you are making right now. Celebrate the small efforts you are taking to heal from childhood traumas and past relationship mistakes. Cheer yourself on, and be the parent that you needed when you were a kid!

3. Believing that your future is hopeless

Beware of limiting beliefs that attempt to paint a negative outlook on the future. Beliefs such as "I will never find love again," or "I can't maintain healthy relationships" can make you feel anxious about starting over again and rebuilding your life. It is important to believe in your ability to unlearn trauma-informed behaviors and live the kind of positive and healthy lifestyle you desire. Continue to recite your positive affirmations, confronting limiting beliefs, and journal about difficult emotions that are uncomfortable to express in words. Constantly reaffirm your needs—especially your emotional needs—so you can take your power back and assume responsibility for your own happiness.

Avoiding blame, shame, and adopting a negative outlook on the future is only one way to cope with post-breakup grief. Another way is to find positive coping strategies to take your mind off the relationship. A few suggestions include:

- **Reach out to your friends and family.** Your social relationships are vital when healing from a painful breakup. Focus on the strong bonds with some of your close friends and family, particularly those relationships that feel emotionally safe. Share your thoughts and feelings, as well as aspects of your codependent relationship you are having a difficult time making peace with.
- **Prioritize your health.** Improve your overall moods by practicing healthy habits like getting proper sleep, eating healthy foods, and working out at least three times a week. Putting your health first can also boost your confidence and make you feel excited about this new chapter in your life.
- **Download a self-care app.** To keep yourself in a good headspace, incorporate self-care techniques into your daily routine. A powerful app that can show you is called Calm. The app allows you to focus on a number of self-care goals, like improving sleep, reducing stress and anxiety, or improving focus—to name a few—and keep

track of your progress and milestones.
- **Create a post-break up music playlist.** Music has the ability to reduce stress and enhance positive moods. Get your phone out and create a one-of-a-kind post-breakup playlist. Keep the theme upbeat and motivational, so you can forget about the breakup blues.
- **Allow yourself to cry, yell, and scream.** Part of the process of healing and recovering from a breakup is being able to process and let go of strong emotions. Create a safe space to express heavy emotions and feel the sense of loss. You don't need to be strong or keep it together during your recovery. It is okay to mourn, and continue mourning until you feel ready to embrace your new life.

Ending ties with a codependent relative, friend, or significant other is painful. Even though your relationship had become toxic, there was still a great deal of love there that caused you to have faith in things getting better. At the end, you decided to choose a happy and healthy life, instead of a life based on false hope. This decision wasn't easy, but it marks the beginning of a brand-new life, living under brand-new terms.

9

Celebrate This New Chapter

"We must be willing to get rid of the life we've planned, so as to have the life that is waiting for us. The old skin has to be shed before the new one can come."

— JOSEPH CAMPBELL

What Are You Looking Forward To?

It is tempting to reminisce about the past when you are beginning a new journey. As painful as the past chapter of your life was, it felt familiar. Now that you are on a different path, you may feel unprepared and anxious about the future.

However, perspective is everything when you are seeking to have a fresh start!

Decide, right now, what your future is going to look like. Are you going to be miserable? Go back to old patterns of behavior? Attract the same quality of men and women that you have been attracting in the past?

Your answer should be a big and bold "NO!"

If you are adamant that this next chapter of your life is not going to look or feel like the last one, then you must change your mentality. When you think differently, you move differently, and as a result, attract different things.

The best way to change your mentality is to set aspirational goals that become the new focus of your life. These goals paint a picture of the quality of life you intend on creating for yourself. It doesn't matter what others might think about your goals. All that matters is that they align with your values and make your life feel meaningful.

There are five steps that you can practice to set aspirational goals that give you something to look forward to:

Step 1: Make a Decision

For once and for all—decide on what you want and why you want it. Be absolutely clear about the intention behind your goal because that is what will keep you going on the journey. Ensure that the goal is a reflection of your desire, and not something that was inspired by someone else. A trick to figuring out if you have found the right goal is to ask yourself: *Would I regret not achieving this goal?*

Take some time to think about your goal and write it down below:

_____

_____

Step 2: Break Down Your Goal

This step is extremely crucial to making sure your goal doesn't overwhelm you. Break down your goal into smaller tasks that can be done on a daily, weekly, and monthly basis. Each task should be simple, easy to practice, and written as an instruction. Note that the less time-consuming and complicated your tasks, the less resistance you will feel to commit.

Use the table below to break down your goal and divide it into daily, weekly, and monthly tasks.

Daily Tasks	Weekly Tasks	Monthly Tasks

Step 3: Plan Your First Step

Now that you know what to focus on throughout the month, decide on your first step. Make sure that the first task is small enough to practice on any given day, with minimum resources required. After successfully completing it, plan your next small task.

Which task will break the ice and mark the beginning of this journey for you?

_____

_____

_____

Step 4: Review Progress Regularly

Choose a day of the week or month that will become the "check-in" day. On that specific day, review the progress you have made for that period, as well as obstacles that you have encountered, so you can decide if a goal adjustment is necessary. The process of pursuing a goal should be challenging, but never demanding.

If you need to reduce the number of goal-related tasks completed monthly, feel free to do so! However, if you don't believe you are being challenged enough, find ways to increase the expectations for each task. For example, instead of working out for 15 minutes, twice per week, you can increase the intensity and workout for 30 minutes, three times per week.

Step 5: Celebrate Your Wins

Make it a point to acknowledge small and big wins. Take a moment to reflect on how far you have come, and what it took to achieve that victory. You can also express gratitude to the people you have played a role in helping you achieve the milestone. Celebrating your wins is what makes the journey worthwhile, so enjoy this small or big achievement!

Nurture Your Close Relationships

No matter how solid a relationship, when it isn't given the right amount of nurturing, it can start to fall apart. In this new chapter of your life, make a decision to prioritize close relationships with friends and family, so you can be rewarded with deep and satisfying connections.

The good news is that since you already have established close relationships, you won't need to start from scratch and get to know your loved ones. However, you may need to practice healthy habits that promote stronger and more fulfilling relationships. Below are five ways to nurture close relationships:

1. Listen with curiosity

Listening is a sign of respect and kindness. It also shows the other person that you care about what they are saying, which makes them feel seen and accepted. When listening, focus attentively on what the other person is saying. Tell yourself that nothing else matters besides what you are hearing. Pause before speaking, and process what you have heard. Truly appreciate their perspective and challenge yourself to learn something new!

2. Be intentional about spending quality time

Connections are maintained through spending quality time together. This doesn't need to be face-to-face interactions; they can also be online catch-ups through video chat or group messaging. If you tend to forget about your loved ones when your schedule gets busy, block out time in your calendar for uninterrupted quality time. Depending on each relationship, how you spend quality time will look different. Some of the suggestions you can consider are:

- coffee dates
- weekly date nights
- family picnics
- going on vacation together
- watching a movie together
- meeting for mentor-mentee appointments

When spending quality time with loved ones, be fully present. Put your devices away (or on silent) and put away as many distractions as possible. It is important for them to feel as though they have your undivided attention, and you have theirs.

3. Notice positive things and express gratitude

It is normal to start taking loved ones for granted because of how comfortable you are in the relationship. However, if you are not careful, you can start to neglect their core needs. Everybody desires to be recognized for their positive contributions—including your loved ones. Take the time to notice something good about them, each time you get together, and show appreciation.

Think about someone who has played an important part in your codependency recovery. It could be a cousin, friend, or colleague, who has always been there to listen and offer advice. Write a gratitude letter to them, mentioning how thankful you are for their support.

Your close relationships make up the core of your support system. These are the people who keep you grounded, offer emotional support, and help you through difficult times. Never miss an opportunity to show them how much significance they hold in your life.

How to Manage the First Healthy Romantic Relationship

An unhealthy relationship can change your perspective on love and closeness. You may doubt that it is possible to build friendships or romantic relationships that feel healthy and supportive. Well, the truth is that there are millions of good people out there, who are capable of meeting you halfway and consciously building healthy relationships with you.

When meeting someone new, you have an opportunity to start off with a solid and healthy foundation. How you approach the relationship—and the values and boundaries you communicate—will set the tone for what kind of dynamic both of you will create. It is therefore critical to decide, ahead of time, what kind of romantic relationship you want moving forward, as well as what standards you will enforce.

The first step in deciding what kind of romantic relationship you want is being clear and resolute about the kind of relationship you DON'T want. Create a list of unacceptable behaviors that are immediate dealbreakers or turn-offs. Examples of unacceptable behaviors include:

- yelling
- playing victim
- physical attacks
- name-calling
- silent treatment
- excessive jealousy
- not being supportive
- threatening to leave
- gaslighting
- controlling

Now that you know what you don't want, consider some of the standards that you will enforce. Remember that standards are not wishes, they are needs that make you feel safe, respected, loved, and supported in your romantic relationships. When these standards are not met, you may suffer emotional distress, like feeling anxious, neglected, or taken for granted.

Below is an example of some of the standards you can set and communicate in your new romantic relationships:

- I must feel attracted to the person.
- I must respect the person.
- I must feel safe around the person.
- I must feel wanted by the person.
- I must feel comfortable expressing my needs.
- I must feel safe sharing my thoughts and feelings.
- The person must believe in equality in a relationship.
- The person must show willingness to respect my boundaries.
- The person must respect my time with friends and family.
- The person must have separate hobbies and interests from mine.
- The person must be a positive influence in my life.

_____
_____
_____
_____
_____

Take another look at your list and identify five non-negotiable standards. These are the standards that are mandatory in order to continue getting to know someone. Be mindful of these standards whenever you meet new people.

Rewrite Your Life Story

In Chapter 7, we spoke a little about negative life stories that produce limiting beliefs. But in this final section, we are going to take a closer look at these negative life stories and put a positive spin on them—one story at a time.

Just to recap, life stories are created after going through various experiences and drawing life lessons from them. Depending on how you perceived those experiences back then, you created empowering or disempowering stories.

It is important to identify life stories that are disempowering, so that you can reflect on those past experiences again and reframe them positively. Being able to look back on your life and find the goodness in everything that you have been through can be the kind of encouragement you need to face current challenges.

Below are five practical ways to rewrite disempowering life stories and regain control of your life. But before you go into them, write down your current life story below:

_____

_____

_____

_____

1. Challenge negativity bias

Negativity bias is the process of focusing on the negative aspects of a situation and overlooking or downplaying the positive aspects. Human brains are wired to do this naturally, so you will need to make a deliberate attempt to catch yourself when a life story starts to sound too negative.

Rewrite your life story and challenge yourself to find the silver lining of that situation, something positive that you can appreciate.

2. Change roles

Consider which movie "role" you play in your own story. For instance, are you the supporting actor or the main actor? Do you take orders from someone, or do you give orders? If your current story portrays you as anything other than the main actor, switch roles.

Rewrite your life story to highlight your strengths, victories, and talents. Read the new narrative and notice how you feel. Do you feel like a hero? If not, take another look to see if you have cast yourself in the right role.

3. Allow opportunity for change

Rewrite your life story to allow opportunities for change. If your previous story made your life outcomes seem final, adjust them to allow for positive improvements in the future. For example, you can change "I wasted my youth making bad choices" to "I spent my youth learning what I didn't want in life, so I can live my adult years as I wish."

4. Create a new theme

What is the current theme of your life story? Does it motivate you to continue working on personal growth? Or does it feel discouraging? Look at your story from a fresh angle. See the possibilities where you once saw limitations. Create a new theme that inspires positive action and a continued effort to heal from past experiences.

5. Create a happy ending to defeat the villain

Often in movies, the villain is the character that is attempting to sabotage the hero. In your life, various people or self-destructive behaviors have played the role of villain. For many years, it seemed as though the villain was winning, but recently (when you began your codependency recovery journey), the hero remembered their own strength!

Change the ending of your life story to reflect the better position you are in right now. Show a change in how you present the villain; from being an undefeatable monster to an enemy that you have overcome!

Strengthen Your Relationship With the Divine

If you are spiritually inclined, or are at least curious to learn more about spirituality, you can make an effort to strengthen your relationship with the Divine. Spirituality is about embracing the fullness of life and allowing yourself to be guided. People have different views regarding who or what guides them, but for the purpose of this section, we will call that energy or entity, Divine.

The benefit of connecting to the Divine, especially after coming out of a codependent relationship, is to understand the meaning of life, and which direction you seek to take. Since the Divine represents infinite wisdom, it has the ability to guide you toward people, places, and opportunities that are aligned to your values, beliefs, and talents.

Growing up, you may have often felt a lack of guidance, particularly from the people who you trusted the most to provide a sense of security. For example, not being able to approach your parents about important conversations related to things like identity, puberty, sex and intimacy, or pursuing life goals, caused you to rely on your peers or the media to search for knowledge.

Looking back, you may agree that if you had proper guidance, perhaps you wouldn't have felt so alone, confused, or unprepared for life. Even though you cannot redo the past, it is possible to receive the guidance you have always longed for, by connecting to your higher power. The kind of guidance you are able to receive from the Divine can assist you with:

- Processing and releasing past trauma.
- Healing unhealthy attachments.
- Silencing the voice of the ego, so you can receive divine inspiration.
- Making important life transitions that can be terrifying.
- Healing the inner child and learning healthier patterns of relating to others.
- Living a life that is aligned to your values and beliefs.

Your ability to grow spiritually and connect to the Divine depends on your level of openness to change. The closer you get to the all-knowing, all-powerful entity, the more self-awareness you will gain. You will feel empowered to confront unhealthy habits and beliefs with compassion, and redefine who you are, what you desire most out of life, and the kinds of relationships you seek to build.

If you are ready to take this spiritual journey and connect to your higher power, below are a few spiritual practices you can try:

- **Practice silent meditation**

The moment you open your eyes, before getting out of bed, take five minutes to practice a silent meditation. The only thing you need to do is lie down on your back, close your eyes, and breathe. Allow the silence and gentle bringing to raise your consciousness and help you connect to a deeper part of yourself. If there are any inspired thoughts that come to your mind during this time, make a mental note, then write them down in a notebook afterward.

- **Practice manifesting Divine energy**

The Divine is an energy or entity that doesn't have a shape or form. However, on an energetic level, you can sense the presence of the Divine. It can feel like witnessing someone you love walk inside a room and brighten up the place with their smile. The warm, nurturing, and strong energy you feel whenever you are doing something you love, helping others, or witnessing a work of art is a sign that you have manifested Divine energy. Spend more time practicing activities that manifest that warm, nurturing, and strong energy within you. Find at least one hobby that provides this opportunity for you.

- **Be mindful of how you are being guided**

Tapping into your gut instinct, or intuition, can help you notice the various ways the Divine guides you. The form of guidance can be very specific, such as seeing images or symbols, hearing distinct sounds, having vivid dreams, or having miracle encounters with strangers. Look for the synchronicities, or patterns, between the guidance you receive and the real-life events or challenges you are faced with. Moreover, learn to take notes of signs that you believe have a deeper meaning.

- **Be available for guidance**

It is difficult to connect with the Divine when your mind has wandered to the past or future. Since Divine energy embodies pure consciousness, it is always available in the present moment. In order to connect to the Divine, you must also be present and focus on what is happening right now, right here. Practicing grounding techniques or meditation can help you cultivate presence and reduce mind-wandering.

- **Practice gratitude**

Divine energy is abundant energy. This means that when you trust in your higher power to take care of you, you can rest assured that goodness will find you, and every problem will have a solution or positive outcome. Therefore, cultivate an environment in your life where you are constantly thankful for what you have, or the experiences you are going through (even the challenging ones). Visualize every obstacle or opportunity working out favorably for you.

This new chapter of your life is going to be extraordinary. What will make it extraordinary are the positive actions that you will take to live a life that you never imagined was possible. Mourn the loss of the old you, along with relationships that had to be cut off. Show gratitude for those painful times that have taught you how to stand up for yourself and regain control over your life. Everything happens for a reason. Believe that the reason is always favorable to you!

Conclusion

"Holding on is believing that there's only a past; letting go is knowing that there's a future."

— DAPHNE ROSE KINGMA

The moment you realize that a relationship has become toxic, you are presented with an ultimatum: save the relationship or save yourself.

As someone living with codependency issues, who has been conditioned since childhood to put others' needs first, your initial choice may be to save the relationship. After all, who else can take care of others better than you? But after going through this book and learning about the value of self-care and enforcing boundaries to protect your needs, you may end up saving yourself.

It is important to take a moment and recognize how much of a big deal it is to finally come to a place where you can choose yourself. Many years ago, the thought of putting yourself first could have made you feel selfish.

Throughout your life, your focus has been on rescuing other people from their own personal dramas. The role of being a giver was forced upon you, before you were old enough to choose. Perhaps you were raised by a workaholic, alcoholic, or mentally ill parent, who relied on you to mature quickly and take care of the household in their absence, or provide emotional support for their needs.

As a result, the subconscious message you learned was that it was unacceptable to share your thoughts and express your longing for affection. What many people don't understand about putting others first is that it can make you feel invisible. There is only so much time, money, and energy you can give to others, before you start feeling drained and resentful for not getting the same effort and support given to you.

The road to codependency recovery is marked by the four stages that you will need to go through: abstinence, awareness, acceptance, and action. These four stages will support you in recognizing and healing unhealthy attachments, reaffirming your needs, and building safe relationships where you are able to express who you are without fear of rejection or judgment. During recovery, you are able to confront limiting beliefs, poor boundaries, and obsessive tendencies that make it difficult to form healthy and stable relationships with others.

Your openness to learning new information about yourself is what makes recovery possible. Unless you are able to challenge the current status quo in your life, you may struggle to adopt healthier patterns of behavior. Continue to lead with curiosity, and reflect on tough questions that get you to think about the "why" and the "how": *Why do I behave this way? How can I address it?*

CONCLUSION

To recap, here are the nine chapters (and strategies) presented in this book:

1. Define Codependency
2. Understand the Risk Factors
3. Recognize How Codependency Looks in Different Relationships
4. End the Terror of Obsessive Thinking
5. Put Yourself First and Set Boundaries
6. Learn the Art of Assertive Communication
7. Improve Your Relationship With Fear
8. Decide to Stay or Leave
9. Celebrate This New Chapter

The knowledge gained from these nine chapters is enough to support you on this amazing recovery journey. Feel free to flip through the pages of this book, whenever you need a reminder of who you are and the incredible life you deserve.

If you have found this book valuable, please leave a review. I would love to hear about your progress!

BONUS: Your Free Gifts

I'm only offering this bonus for FREE to my readers. This is a way of saying thanks for your purchase. In this gift, you will find a self-development course to give your inner journey a head start.

The Personality Development Wisdom Course

Master the Art of Becoming the Best Version of Yourself for **Ultimate Succes and Growth!**

BONUS: YOUR FREE GIFTS

Inside this course, you will find:

1. Personality Development - An Overview
2. How to Transform Yourself into a Better Version
3. How To Improve Your Body Language
4. How to Boost Up Your Self-Confidence, Self-Esteem, and Motivation
5. Best Tips to Overcome Procrastination
6. The Power of Positive Thinking
7. How to Improve Your Workplace Wellness
8. How to Enhance Your Softskill
9. Learn and Practice the Art of Work-Life Balance
10. How to Deal With Failures
11. How to Manage and Overcome Your Fears
12. Best Ways to Deal With Difficult People
13. Stress and Energy Management
14. How to Have a Productive Day
15. Bonus 1 - Cheat Sheet
16. Bonus 2 - Mind Map
17. Bonus 3 - Top Resource Report
18. Bonus 4 - 10 Extra Articles

To receive this extra **bonus,** go to: https://booksforbetterlife.com/codependency-recovery-workbook

Or scan the QR code:

CODEPENDENCY RECOVERY WORKBOOK

Thank You

I really appreciate you for purchasing my book!

You had the chance to pick many other books, but you chose this one.

So, **thank you so much** for purchasing this book and reading it to the very last page! I hope that I was able to help you in your healing process, as my goal is to help as many people as possible!

Before you close the book, I want to ask for **a small favor**. Would you please consider *leaving an honest review* about the book? **This would be really helpful for me**, as I'm an independent author and posting reviews is the best and easiest way to support me.

The review you provide will help me so I can continue selling, improving, and writing books. **It will mean the world to me to hear from you.**

Go to this book and scroll down (https://mybook.to/codependency-recovery), or scan the QR code to leave a review:

CODEPENDENCY RECOVERY WORKBOOK

Amazon US <— —> Amazon UK

Amazon CA <— —> Amazon AU

References

Cherry, K. (2022, May 2). *What is attachment theory?* Verywell Mind. https://www.verywellmind.com/what-is-attachment-theory-2795337

Chopra, D. (2013, August 9). *How to communicate your emotional needs in relationships.* Chopra. https://chopra.com/articles/how-to-identify-and-express-your-needs-in-relationships

Christiansen, L. (2020, July 30). *What is an obsessive personality? Signs, symptoms and treatments.* Straight Talk Clinic. https://www.straighttalkcounseling.org/post/what-is-an-obsessive-personality-signs-symptoms-treatments-by-lauren-christiansen

Lancer, D. (2022, July 2). *What is a trauma bond?* What Is Codependency? https://whatiscodependency.com/what-is-a-trauma-bond/

Moulik, S. (2022, April 25). *Individuation process: Learn to master your "self" in 5 stages.* Change Your Mind Change Your Life. https://medium.com/change-your-mind/individuation-process-learn-to-master-your-self-in-5-stages-52ac89b19ce7

Printed in Great Britain
by Amazon